MIRACULOUS
WONDERS

By

Cecelia Frances Page

iUniverse, Inc.
New York   Bloomington

MIRACULOUS WONDERS

iUniverse books may be ordered through booksellers or by contacting:

iUniverse
1663 Liberty Drive
Bloomington, IN 47403
www.iuniverse.com
1-800-Authors (1-800-288-4677)

Because of the dynamic nature of the Internet, any Web addresses or links contained in this book may have changed since publication and may no longer be valid. The views expressed in this work are solely those of the author and do not necessarily reflect the views of the publisher, and the publisher hereby disclaims any responsibility for them.

ISBN: 978-1-4502-3680-5 (sc)
ISBN: 978-1-4502-3681-2 (ebk)

Printed in the United States of America

iUniverse rev. date: 06/17/2010

Contents

Preface

MIRACULOUS WONDERS is a fascinating and worthwhile book with 65 short stories and articles. HUMAN INTEREST TOPICS are The Eccentric Individual, The Skaters, Shelley's Baby, Herman's Telescope, The Shoe Factory, Neighborly Deeds, The Birthday Cards, Robin's Choices, Contemporary Superstars, Fond Memories, Danielle The Seamstress, Romance During A Journey, Felicity Meets Alex in The Fourth Dimension, The Journalist and The Enlightened Poet.

ADVENTURE TOPICS are Swiss Pilot Takes To The Skies, Traveling In A Trailer, Raptures At Ebb Tide, Unusual Dreams, Traveling Adventures, Adventures At Sea and Walking Adventures.

SCIENTIFIC, NATURE and HEALTH TOPICS are Healthy Exercises For The Brain, Scientists Observe Space Spheres, Titan's Weather Is Almost Earth-like, Let's Preserve Earth's Trees, Eclipses, Microscopes Are Valuable, The Nearby Pond, Cats Have Unusual Perception, Different Kinds Of Energy, Insects

Respond, Healing Power, Encounter With A Space Being, Awareness About Nature, Bear Country, Zebras Are Interesting, The Vegetarian Banquet, Intergalactic Experiences, Snow Country, Training Elephants and The Healing Spring.

HISTORICAL and POLITICAL TOPICS are The Emancipation, Historical Awareness About Greece and The American Economy. MUSIC and ARTISTIC TOPICS are The Artist's Studio, Melodrama Experience, Concentric Rings, Tango Dancing, Some Musical Instruments, The Special Photographs, Participating In An Orchestra and Music Can Uplift You. PHILOSOPHICAL and MYSTICAL TOPICS are Awakenings, Transparent Reality, Metaphysics Will Enlighten You, Unusual Dreams and Reincarnation Exists. OTHER TOPICS are Bogus Sweepstakes Prizes Are Scams, An Imaginary Experience, Bedtime Stories and Wonders In The World.

Cecelia Frances Page

About the Author

Cecelia Frances Page has a B.A. and M.A. in Education. She also focused in English, Speech, Drama, Psychology and Music. Cecelia is a prolific writer of original poems, screenplays, novels and nonfiction books. Forty-three of Cecelia's books are published by iUniverse Incorporated. Cecelia has published five, original screenplays and three, original, poetry books. Cecelia Frances Page is an educator, author, drama director, pianist, vocal soloist, artist, photographer and philosopher. Cecelia Frances Page continues to write worthwhile and inspirational books. She has written 52 books.

Novels written by Cecelia Frances Page are *WESTWARD PURSUIT, IMAGINE IF...,OPPORTUNE TIMES, MYSTICAL REALITIES, BRILLIANT CANDOR, SEEK ENLIGHTENMENT WITHIN, CELESTIAL CONNECTIONS, CELESTIAL BEINGS FROM OUTER SPACE, PATHWAYS TO SELF REALIZATION, MAGNIFICENT CELESTIAL JOURNEYS, EXTRAORDINARY ENCOUNTERS, HORIZONS BEYOND,*

PHENOMENAL EXPERIENCES, ADVENTURES ON ANCIENT CONTINENTS And *FORTUNATELY*.

<u>Philosophical and Religious Book</u> are *AWAKEN TO SPIRITUAL ILLUMINATION, EXPAND YOUR AWARENESS, VIVID MEMORIES OF HALCYON. MYSTICAL REALITIES AND PATHWAYS TO SPIRITUAL REALIZATION*.

<u>Cecelia Frances Page's Books of Short Stories and Articles</u> are: *INCREDIBLE TIMES, FASCINATING TOPICS, INTERPRETATIONS OF LIFE, ADVENTUROUS EXPERIENCES, MARVELOUS REFLECTIONS, STIMULATING AWARENESS ABOUT LIFE, MAGNIFICENT RECOLLECTIONS, MIRACULOUS WONDERS, CERTAIN PEOPLE MAKE A DIFFERENCE, VERY WORTHWHILE ENDEAVORS AND CIRCUMSTANCES, POWER OF CREATIVE AND WORTHWHILE LIVING, AWESOME EPISODES, NEW PERSPECTIVES, TREMENDOUS MOMENTS, AMAZING STORIES AND ARTICLES, RELEVANT INTERESTS, IMPRESSIONABLE OCCURRENCES, INFINITE OPPORTUNITIES, RANDOM SELECTIONS, SIGNIFICANT MOMENTS, IMMENSE POSSIBILITIES, AUTHENTIC INSIGHTS* and more.

<u>Nonfiction Books</u> are *REMARKABLE WORLD TRAVELS, THE FUTURE AGE BEYOND THE NEW AGE MOVEMENT* and *EXTRATERRESTRIAL CIVILIZATIONS ON EARTH*.

Fiction

ONE

The Golden Key

Ezelda Sherman lived in a large, stone castle on a high hill in Ireland. She had long red hair, blue eyes and she was tall and slim. Ezelda lived during the 12th century before the New World was discovered. She walked around the enormous, stone castle. There were many closed, locked doors and dark passages in the castle.

Ezelda was curious about what was behind many locked doors. She looked for keys to unlock the many sealed off doors. Ezelda looked in drawers and key hooks for the right keys to unlock the doors. She was unable to locate keys that would unlock these many doors.

Days and weeks went by and Ezelda kept searching without finding keys which would unlock each door. She began to become discouraged. She went outside and roamed in the verdant-green countryside near the castle. She saw deer and their fawns nibbling grass in the meadows near the castle. Ezelda heard robins, meadowlarks and sparrows chirping in the nearby trees.

Ezelda continued to walk in the rich green meadow. She stopped occasionally to smell buttercups, aliciums and four leaf clovers. She approached a brook and walked into the splashing, flowing, fresh, blue water. The moving water was cool and refreshing. It was springtime and life around the countryside near the castle was new and beautiful.

Several red foxes appeared in the meadow not far from Ezelda. They appeared to be searching for bird eggs in the grass and nearby brush. Ezelda observed the foxes with their bushy tails. They crawled into a hollow log in the meadow after searching for the bird eggs. Ezelda continued to roam in the countryside. She had stopped thinking about the locked castle doors briefly.

As Ezelda was walking further she heard a strange sound coming from the pine tree forest near the meadow. She decided to walk over to the forest to find out more about who was making the strange sounds. As she walked deeper into the forest the sounds became louder. Ezelda kept walking slowly and cautiously under the tall, fragrant pine trees.

Suddenly a large hawk appeared in the distance. It made more strange sounds. The hawk flew from one branch to another branch. Then it fluttered its wings several times. The hawk saw Ezelda approaching it. The hawk flew much higher in a tall pine tree and perched on a high limb. Ezelda stopped and stared at it. Ezelda had seen hawks before. She wasn't afraid of the hawk.

Ezelda decided to rest. She sat down under a tall pine tree in the shade. She looked up at the brown hawk. It was still perching on the high limb. It stopped making sounds. So, Ezelda rested quietly for awhile. She fell into a deep sleep.

While Ezelda was sleeping she began to dream. She dreamt about finding a golden key which could be used to unlock all the doors in the castle. The key was a bright shiny gold. She dreamt that she returned to the castle and that she used the golden key to open each door in the castle. As Ezelda unlocked one door at a time she looked into empty, spacious rooms. She walked into each room and looked around. Most of the castle rooms were empty.

Finally, Ezelda unlocked a door which led to a golden room with a lot of sunlight beaming into it from different windows. She saw beautiful, wooden dolls dressed in magnificent costumes. The dolls were lying on a big bed. The bed was covered with a cheerful, purple bedspread. Above the bed was a canopy with a white curtain dropping around the side of the bed. Each doll was carefully placed on the big bed.

Ezelda saw little children come into the room. They went over to play with the elegant dolls. The children were very preoccupied with the dolls. They didn't seem to notice Ezelda standing in the room. It was as if she wasn't in the room. Ezelda wondered why the children didn't notice her. They kept playing with the dolls.

One of the children was dominating the other children. She was telling them to give her the dolls.

They refused to give them to her. She argued with them. Ezelda became concerned that this girl was disturbing the other girls. She decided to speak to the girl who was dominating the group of girls. Ezelda said, "Why are you causing the other girls to be uncomfortable? There are enough dolls to share. Stop bothering the other girls!" The girl looked at Ezelda and she wondered why Ezelda was in the room. The girl looked concerned because she was being scolded by Ezelda. She frowned and looked unhappy. Finally she said, "Who are you? Why are you here? I have never seen you before! These are my dolls! I have a right to play with them!"

Ezelda said, "Learn to share your dolls. You should be willing to let these girls play with them, too." The girl stared at Ezelda coldly. She replied, "I have a right to decide who can play with my dolls! You should mind your own business! I am going to call my mother to ask you to leave!" The little girl started calling for her mother. Within minutes the little girl's mother entered the room.

The mother was not familiar with Ezelda. Ezelda recognized the mother. Ezelda spoke to the mother and she told her how her daughter was unwilling to share her dolls. The mother looked at her daughter, who was called Gilda. The mother said, "Gilda, you should share your dolls with the other girls! If you don't share them I will take them away!"

Gilda burst out in tears and cried. She didn't want to share her dolls. So, the mother started collecting the dolls. Gilda cried out, "Please don't take my dolls away!"

The mother looked at Gilda sternly and said, "If you are willing to share them with the other girls I won't take them away!"

Gilda still had tears in her eyes. However, she decided to listen to her mother and obey her. She didn't want her dolls taken away. Gilda handed dolls to the other girls. She stopped bickering about them. She allowed the girls to play with them. Her mother thanked Ezelda and then she left the room. The girls went on playing with the elegant looking dolls.

Ezelda suddenly woke up and realized she had been dreaming. It was getting dark. She noticed that the hawk had appeared on the high limb. Ezelda stood up and began walking out of the forest. She walked back into the meadow. She walked towards the castle. She entered the castle and walked around. She tried opening the doors in the castle. She saw a key lying near one of the doors. She decided to pick up the key to try to unlock the castle doors. Ezelda was surprised when she used the key to unlock the doors. She was able to unlock the doors with this one key. Ezelda went back to her own room, which was beautifully furnished and sunny. At least, she was able to unlock the doors in the castle at last!

TWO

Healthy Exercises For The Brain

Dr. Eve Clute, Doctor of Public Health, has given health tips about exercising the brain. She said, "The brain is composed of three sections. The neocortex is where high level thinking and complex, integrative tasks take place." If we use our brain to think of creative ideas and to stimulate our minds with higher consciousness we can maintain an alert awareness of life.

Dr. Eve Clute said, "The limbic system generates the emotions, memory, appetite and survival urges." If we maintain balance and equilibrium we can help maintain a much healthier brain. We retain our memory by recalling past experiences, places, people and special events.

"The cerebellum regulates basic vital variables such as breathing, heartbeat and motor coordination," said Dr. Eve Clute. It is important how to breathe properly. Deep breaths expand the lungs. More oxygen sent into one's body oxidizes the body cells. Our heartbeat is regulated by maintaining balance and positive body rhythm. We need to exercise by walking, running and even jogging. Motor coordination is vital because body movements should be coordinated step by step.

Dr. Eve Clute said," The brain keeps developing, no matter what your age is." We continue to learn as we grow. So, our brain keeps developing as we grow. Dr. Eve Clute said, "Researchers have long known that the brain's processing speed gradually slows as we age. Between age 25 and 55, we're likely to lose about 25 percent of our synapses, the connections that relay messages from neuron to neuron." You have observed that some elderly people are very alert and retain their memories. Yet, many elderly people have less dexterity and stamina. Many elderly people are not physically strong and capable of strenuous, physical experiences.

Dr. Eve Clute stated that "A vigorous physical workout triggers parts of the brain related to movement and balance, which can keep neuron connections strong. Activities that exercise our body can also help sharpen our brain. Physical exercise enhances neurogenesis." Our nervous system affects our brain. The more we stimulate our brain with physical exercises the more we become alert and mentally aware.

Our brain continues to develop with new neuronal cells from birth throughout adult life. Even the hippocampus, which processes short-term memory and awareness of one's environment, affects our brain by developing neurogenesis.

It is known that physical exercise increases circulation which causes your body to pump nutrient and oxygen-rich blood to your brain. Dr. Eve Clute claims that "adequate blood flow to the brain is also necessary for nerve cell growth."

Stress causes tension in the brain. So, we need to exercise in order to decrease stress, which can affect one's long-term memory. Cortisol, the stress hormone, limits the number of cells in the hippocampus, where the memory is stored in the brain.

Neurons are killed by stress and anxiety because brain cells become imbalanced. Anxiety and stress prevents the creation of new neurons according to Dr. Eve Clute. "When we mentally exercise our brains, we put our neurons in action. Neurons must have a purpose to survive. Without a purpose, neurons die through a process called apoptosis, in which neurons that do not receive or transmit information become damaged and die," Dr. Eve Clute stated.

You can exercise your brain by working on crossword puzzles and playing brain-enhancing games on the Internet. You can participate in discussion groups, develop vocabulary and perform in debates, etc.

Nonfiction

THREE

Scientists Observe Space Spheres

Susan Jamison claims that "mysterious space-age spheres found buried in ancient rock formations have led astonished experts to conclude that intelligent, alien, life forms roamed the Earth over 2,800 million years ago and even mined diamonds." What are these miniature spheres? Where do they come from? These are questions that need to be answered.

Susan Jamison describes the polished metal globes which have three parallel grooves. She claims the spheres could only have been made by a technologically advanced society. They have been found in rocks 30 million centuries before man existed on Earth.

Museum curator, Rolf Marx of Klerksdorp Museum from South Africa said, "The spheres are a complete mystery. They look man-made." Yet, spheres existed in very ancient rocks before humanity dwelled on the Earth. This is a mystery. Rolf Marx said, "They're like nothing I have ever seen before." He discovered the spheres revolve slowly on their axis, like small planets. He stated, "In a year, a sphere will make a complete revolution or two. But we simply can't explain how or why this happens."

"It's perfectly possible that the metal balls were made by space aliens," said Mrs. Brenda Sullivan, head of a noted South African Society that studies ancient archaeological findings. It is possible that a higher civilization in ancient times made the mysterious spheres. Spheres are found all over the world. They don't fit in with the time period in which they were buried. Their ability to rotate slowly is uncanny.

Susan Jamison has suggested that "A psychic should examine them." She stated, "A number of experts theorize that the metal balls landed in South America like a meteor shower from outer space. But others believe that space aliens actually brought them to Earth on an expedition." There is speculation about who brought the spheres to Earth.

FOUR

The American Economy

The American economy has been gradually falling because the American dollar has lost considerable value. Thomas Jefferson, (1743-1826) a United States President, stated, "I believe that banking institutions are more dangerous to our liberties than standing armies." What did he mean? He believed banking institutions are dangerous perhaps because they can collapse easily.

Tanya Carina Hsu stated, "The banking industry renamed insurance betting guarantees as "Credit default swaps" and risky gambling wagers as "derivatives." Derivatives are monies taken out of different funds.

Why has the American economy fallen? It began in the early 20th Century when a banker published a false rumor that an unnamed large bank was about to fail. Bankers panicked and withdrew their banking assets out of their banks. This caused many banks to collapse and become bankrupt. The 1907 panic resulted in a crash that encouraged the opening of the Federal Reserve, a private banking cartel. Elite bankers were able to control the American economy.

"The Federal Reserve signed into law in 1913 the opportunity to lend and supply the nation's money. However, with high interest," stated Tanya Carina Hsu. The more money printed caused more income to generate for itself. The Federal Reserve would forever keep producing debt to stay alive. The Federal Reserve has regulated the value of money.

In 1907, when many people pulled out their funds from their banks, the banks lost their cash deposits. They were forced to call in their loans. People were forced to pay back their mortgages to provide the banks with money. It took time for the banks to be restored again.

Tanya Carina Hsu said, "The Federal Reserve then doubled America's money supply within five years." By 1920, 5,000 banks collapsed overnight. In one year the Federal Reserve increased the money supply by 62 percent. Yet, in 1929 the Federal Reserve called the loans in, "en masse." "16,000 banks crashed in 1929. There was an 89 percent "plunge" on the stock market", stated Tanya Carina Hsu. The nation fell into a Great Depression.

In 1933, gold bullions were stopped by President Franklin Roosevelt. Anyone who didn't turn in their gold was imprisoned for 10 years. Thus, gold was no longer used as money. Paper money was used instead. President Richard Nixon removed the dollar from the gold standard altogether," stated Tanya Carina Hsu.

After the Great Depression, Franklin Roosevelt created the Fannie Mae program. Fannie Mae became a state-supported mortgage bank which provided federal funding to finance home mortgages for affordable housing. In 1968, President Lynden Johnson privatized Fannie Mae. "By 1970, Fannie Mae bought mortgages from banks and other lenders and sold them on to new investors," Tanya Carina Hsu stated.

It has been unfortunate that the Fannie Mae mortgages have become corrupt in recent years causing buyers to pay high mortgage payments. Many home buyers who have taken out loans from Fannie Mae have lost their homes because they have not been able to make their regular, monthly mortgage payments. In 2008-2009 big banks were failing because many home loans have not been paid off.

Major banks such as Bank of America, Wells Fargo Bank, Washington Mutual and other banks have gone bankrupt in 2008-2009. President Barrack Obama has tried to restore major banks by giving them millions of dollars from the Federal Reserve Bank. Bank administrators have misused the money they were given.

During the 1990s, the second mortgages became commonplace. Home buyers depended on using their homes for equity and collateral. Chairman Alan Greenspan kept interest rates low. Greenspan's rock-bottom interest rates let anyone afford a home. Minimum wage, service workers were able to secure 100% loans to buy expensive homes.

Tanya Carina Hsu stated, "It has always been the case that a bank would lend out more than it actually had, because interest payments generated its income. The more the bank lent, the more interest it collected--even with no money in the vault. It was a lucrative industry of giving away money in the vault." This was a risky business, especially when there was not enough money in the bank. Tanya Carina Hsu said, "Mortgage banks and investment houses even borrowed money on international money markets to fund these 100 percent plus sub-prime mortgages." So, the banks have had to borrow money to use for loans. This indicates that the banks are unable to finance home loans unless they borrow money.

Tanya Carina Hsu has stated, "The financial industry also believed that housing prices would forever climb, but should they ever fall, the central bank would cut interest rates so that prices would jump back up." The American economy depends on the success of Wall Street Stock Market and restoration of the banking system in America. When enough Americans are working to pay their home loans and living expenses the American economy will improve.

Non-Fiction

FIVE

Titan's Weather Is Almost Earth-Like

Titan is a moon of Saturn with weather that is almost Earth-like. NASA's Jet Propulsion Laboratory in Pasadena, California "Reports that its study of 200 clouds in the lower atmosphere of the frozen moon shows its weather patterns look a bit like Earth's, only slower. Titan's clouds don't move with the seasons exactly as we expected," said Cassini spacecraft mission member, Sebastian Rodriguez of Paris Diderot University in a statement.

Titan is the only moon with a substantial atmosphere in our solar system. The international Cassini spacecraft mission is on an extended tour to study Saturn and its moons. It may be possible for human beings from Earth to live on Titan's surface because there is oxygen.

Rich inorganic material in Titan's atmosphere imparts a smooth, featureless, orange glow. NASA rockets have been sent to Saturn to observe Titan and Saturn.

Europa may have organic life in water. Europa revolves around Jupiter. So, life exists on these moons in our solar system. Titan is farther from the Sun than Europa. Yet, its atmosphere is more developed than Europa's atmosphere. It is possible that life on Titan is more evolved. Saturn is a gaseous planet. Yet, Titan is a solid moon revolving around Saturn.

We need to know our solar system. There are many moons that revolve around Jupiter. Yet, Titan is the only moon which seems to have life, while it rotates around Saturn.

Nonfiction

SIX

Awakenings

We are awakened with sudden flashes of higher awareness. Our higher perceptions can be awakened step by step. For instance, if we gaze at the heavens to witness twinkling stars we can visualize how stars move in outer space. We know the Sun is very bright so its light may be too bright to look at. We can glimpse at the Sun very briefly.

We may awaken to a blissful state of consciousness while we are dreaming or remembering enlightening experiences. Our higher consciousness can expand our outer consciousness to awaken to God consciousness. Awakenings help us grow spiritually. We are able to experience a blissful state of consciousness in order to awaken to Nirvana. Nirvana is a heavenly place of peace and harmony where beings experience degrees of cosmic consciousness and God reality. Magnificent color rays, and pillars of blazing light, flash about in

Nirvana. Celestial sounds and mystical music can be heard. Celestial beings move around freely in Nirvana.

Gautama Buddha, from India, was aware of Nirvana once he became enlightened. He went within with his inner eye to experience this heavenly abode. He experienced higher consciousness and awakenings as he searched for eternal truths and wisdom.

Sages and saints have had awakenings as they pursued cosmic awareness. Confucius, from China, experienced awakenings and higher consciousness. He wrote down words of wisdom.

Awakenings can liberate your soul. The more you learn to relate to your higher self the more you can awaken to wisdom and truth.

SEVEN

Swiss Pilot Takes To The Skies

In Switzerland, Yves Rossy, a Swiss pilot was strapped on a jet powered wing as he leaped from a plane. He was demonstrating a homemade device as he turned figure eights and soared high above the Alps. Yves Rossy had five years of training to be able to fly so high above the Alps.

Yves Rossy said, "This flight was absolutely excellent," once he touched down on an airfield near the eastern shore of Lake Geneva. Rossy, who is 48, had stepped out of the Swiss-built Pilatus Porter aircraft at 7,500 feet. Rossy accelerated to 186 mph which was about 65 mph faster than the typical, descending skydiver.

The rocket man dipped his wings to the crowd as he flipped onto his back and leveled out again, experiencing a perfect 360 degree roll. He impressed the crowd observing below on the ground.

More divers are experimenting in the sky by flying independently. Flying with wings is much more interesting than going down in parachutes or parasailing in the sky. With the proper training, men and women can learn to fly independently in the sky to experience the thrill of viewing the Earth from very high heights.

During ancient civilizations individuals flew in the sky to travel faster from one place to another. They wore miniature motors on the wings. so they could fly long distances across the sky. Today winged men are repeating what ancient, winged men achieved.

Nonfiction

EIGHT

Bogus Sweepstakes Prize Is A Scam

There are many scams which occur frequently around the world. Scammers use the names of different banks such as Bank of America, Wells Fargo Bank and other banks. "There are some very brilliant scammers out there," said Milt Shefter, who is a Beverly Hills resident. Someone tried to get him to pay $850 for a $2.5 million "prize."

"Unfortunately, phony lottery or sweepstakes scams are common," said Jennifer Langan, a bank spokeswoman. "Shefter contacted me after receiving two calls." She said she could hear voices in the background telling other people about their multimillion-dollar winnings.

The fact that advanced fee and bogus-check scams persist, demonstrates their alarmingly high success rate. The Federal Trade Commission says scams involving sweepstakes and counterfeit checks are among the most commonly reported to the agency. The FTC advises to "throw away any offer that asks you to pay for a prize or a gift. If it's free or a gift, you shouldn't have to pay for it. Free is free."

Like the FTC, Chris Irving said, "That if strings are attached to collecting a prize, chances are it's a scam. Walk away. Don't look back". David Lazarus said, "Or do what the Shefters did and string the scammers along as you can. Two can play at that game, after all!"

NINE

Let's Preserve Earth's Trees

We need to preserve trees on the Earth. If trees are constantly cut down this creates an imbalance on Earth. The soil becomes depleted and erosion sets in.

Trees provide protection to the Earth's soil. Trees absorb water and hold soil down with their tree roots. Trees provide shade and a place for creatures to dwell and live. Creatures are protected in and near trees and they feel safer in trees.

Trees provide oxygen to supply the Earth with this necessary air to breathe. We depend on fresh air to survive. Trees should not be chopped down in large quantities. This depletes the environment, which creatures, insects and plants depend on to thrive and grow.

Trees should be planted as much as possible to protect the Earth's environment. Life on Earth will survive much better with an abundance of healthy trees. There are many kinds of trees such as redwood trees, pine and spruce trees, elm and cypress trees, sycamore trees, willow and oak trees, eucalyptus and palm trees and other trees. All of these trees should flourish and grow in large quantities around the Earth. They add to the environments on Earth.

Trees are very valuable. They should be cherished and preserved around the world. Trees enrich the soil and help preserve water as well. We should be grateful to nurture and appreciate trees.

Nonfiction

TEN

The Emancipation

Webster's New Word Dictionary defines emancipation as "to set free such as a slave or to release from bondage, servitude or serfdom." Emancipation also means "to free from restraint or influence, as of convention. There is a law to release a child from parental control and supervision. The Emancipation Proclamation issued by President Abraham Lincoln in September 1862 effective January 1, 1863, freed the slaves in all territories still at war with the Union."

So, emancipation has various meanings. American slaves were able to escape from their slave owners. They escaped at night when their slave owners were sleeping and unaware of their escape. Slave owners often went hunting for escaped slaves. Once they found the slaves they brought them back to their plantations, farms and ranches. These slaves were punished for trying to escape. They were beaten so they wouldn't try to escape again.

Some slaves who escaped, went north where they looked for work. After the 1863 Emancipation, freed slaves worked as sharecroppers. They planted crops and harvested them to survive and make some money to pay their bills. Eventually, freed slaves were allowed to attend schools. They were able to learn to read, write and learn arithmetic.

In time, freed slaves were able to attend trade schools and colleges for black students. They were able to learn different occupations. They became teachers, storekeepers, librarians, secretaries and even nurses, doctors and lawyers.

Ancient Jews were taken into bondage by Egyptians during the time of Ramses II, who was pharaoh of Egypt. Jews were expected to make bricks with mud clay and straw. Jewish slaves made thousands of bricks. They were expected to help build Egyptian pyramids. It took many years to build the pyramids. They worked in severe heat to build these enormous pyramids.

Moses, a Jewish prophet and leader, was forced to leave Egypt. He walked in a nearby desert for 40 days and nights. He finally came to a well. He drank from the well. The daughter of the well owner saw Moses drinking from the well. She came up to Moses and greeted him. Moses was glad to see her.

Moses followed the peasant women to her father's tent. Moses was accepted there. He stayed with them. In time, he married the oldest daughter. One day in years to come Moses was contacted by some angels. He was told to go to Egypt to free the Jews from bondage and slavery.

Moses realized that he had been chosen to liberate the Jews in Egypt. He hesitated to go to Egypt. Aaron, who was a Jew, knew Moses. He encouraged Moses to go to Egypt to free the Jews.

Moses decided to go to Egypt with Aaron to free the Jews. When he entered the pharaoh's palace he walked up to the throne. He spoke to Ramases as he held a rod. He told the pharaoh to release all the Jewish slaves in bondage.

The Egyptian pharaoh refused to release the Jewish slaves. Moses warned the pharaoh that the Egyptians would suffer if the Jews were not freed and released. The pharaoh still refused to free the Jews. Moses demonstrated his rod before the pharaoh. He touched his rod into water. The water turned into blood. The pharaoh still refused to cooperate. Then Moses cast his rod on the floor. It turned into a long snake. The pharaoh didn't let this startle him.

Finally, Moses left the pharaoh's palace. That night the first born of every Egyptian family died. The pharaoh's first child also died. Moses came back to the pharaoh's palace the next day. Moses asked to have the Jews freed. The pharaoh refused to free the Jews. Moses warned the pharaoh again. Then pestilence began after that. Swarms of locusts ate up the crops in the fields. Swarms of insects caused Egyptians to come down with diseases.

Moses came back to the pharaoh's palace in a few days. Moses asked the pharaoh to free the Jews. The pharaoh agreed finally to free the Jews. Moses went to tell the Jews that they were free to leave Egypt. Many of the Jews were afraid to leave Egypt to go out in the desert. Moses finally persuaded everyone to follow him and Aaron to the Promised Land across the desert.

Hundreds of Jews packed their belongings and brought tents. They walked into the desert with Moses. They came to the Red Sea. They began crossing as the water was parted in opposite directions leaving only mud and sand. . They were able to cross the Red Sea. The pharaoh and his Egyptian soldiers chased after the Jews. When every Jew had crossed the opening of the Red Sea the water came back down and drowned the Egyptian soldiers.

The Jews continued traveling across the desert for 40 years. They finally settled in Israel which has been called the Promised Land. The Jews still celebrate Passover. They were emancipated because they were freed from bondage from the Egyptians.

ELEVEN

Eclipses

An eclipse is caused when a shadow is created across the Moon and Sun. When the Moon comes between the Earth and Sun an eclipse takes place. When the Earth blocks the Sun's light from the Moon there is an eclipse.

People during the Middle Ages were superstitious when they witnessed an eclipse of the Moon or the Sun. They became frightened when it became dark. They thought the Sun would no longer shine. People panicked during eclipses.

Eclipses occur when there are alignments between the Moon and Sun to the Earth. Eclipses don't last long. However, it is best not to look at the Sun as the eclipse is moving away from the Sun. The Sun's light is very bright and your eyes can be affected from the Sun's bright, intense light.

Eclipses of the Sun and Moon have occurred at certain times over millions of years. When the Sun and

Moon are in conjunction with the Earth eclipses take place. Fortunately, eclipses do not last long enough to cause harmful conditions to take place on the surface of the Earth.

TWELVE

The Eccentric Individual

Derrick Hanson was an unusual individual. He was outspoken and very opinionated about many topics and issues. He liked to discuss politics, religion and philosophy with his friends and acquaintances.

Derrick majored in Philosophy and Social Science in college. He received his B.S., M.S. and PhD in these subjects. He was an avid reader and he expressed his ideas and opinions clearly. Derrick liked to express his opinions readily.

Friends and acquaintances thought Derrick was eccentric. They thought he was unconventional and somewhat odd. He dressed in old fashion suits and sweaters. He was partially bald and he had piercing eyes. Derrick challenged other people during intellectual discussions. He disagreed with different people about political and religious issues.

Derrick participated in debates at the college where he taught Political Science and Philosophy courses. He was very good at debating. He presented pros and cons about different issues. Derrick was concerned about the American economy. He spoke about what the Illuminati is doing to destroy the money system in America. He spoke up about inflation of the American dollar.

Derrick Hanson wrote articles which were published in various, political magazines. Derrick wrote about problems in the American economy and about the latest health insurance program. He stated solutions to correct the American economy. He suggested that gold and silver be used again to upgrade the value of American money. He mentioned that food and natural resources should be properly distributed and not wasted. Fruits, vegetables and grains are thrown out because farmers are trying to sell certain quantities of their crops at a competitive price. Wasted food is not wise. Many hungry people need food. They could eat the extra food so it would not be wasted.

Derrick believed that low cost housing should be made available for low income families. Lower income people should be able to live in affordable housing throughout the country. The government should provide lower income families with low cost living expenses so these people can live more comfortably. Derrick cared about the welfare of the needy and down and out people.

Derrick spoke up about the need for better education in the public school system. He mentioned that some schools lacked enough educational supplies and equipment which he said is needed to promote a quality education in the schools. He stated the need for a better budget so that teachers could help their students learn better.

Derrick attended school board meetings and PTA (Parent Teacher Association) meetings. He was earnest and sincere about promoting better public schools. He wrote articles about public school education. He stated, "Our children should be taught the three Rs of Reading, Writing and Arithmetic. Every child should receive a good education."

Derrick continued to wear old fashion suits and leather shoes. He grew a beard eventually. He was meticulous about how he decorated and took care of his three bedroom home and garden. He drove a four door sedan Dodge. He seldom ate out. He prepared organic food at his home. He wore bow ties.

Derrick was a rare person because he had unusual interests. He liked to collect ancient relics, old paintings and rare gemstones. He went on hikes and weekend expeditions to search for ancient relics and gemstones. During weekdays he taught college courses at a nearby college in the city where he lived. He had office hours as well in order to help his students.

Derrick didn't let other people push him around. He looked after himself. He had a dog, which stayed in the backyard. Derrick took his dog for walks regularly. Derrick continued to flair up about political issues, education problems and about religious beliefs and concerns. He remained single and devoted his time to his work and writing. He was a humanitarian and tended to be very philosophical. He kept up with current issues in the daily newspapers and on television. His eccentric ways set him apart from other people.

THIRTEEN

Transparent Reality

Transparent reality exists in the world. Reflections of optical illusions intrigue the mind. Images of horizontal and diagonal designs viewed through transparent textures with visible lines fascinate the viewer.

Look into many transparent layers to geometric images to become aware of different artistic visions. Transparent reality amazes the artist who creates unusual designs. Transparent figures become luminous and oblique within transparent dimensions. One can see through transparent textures and substances readily.

Photographers are capable of creating transparent images when they photograph see through images. Shading and light effect transparent designs and objects.

See-through paper, cloth and plastic are transparent, allowing the viewer to see through to the interior images clearly. Parallel planes are invisible, yet seen with the inner eye. Transparent visions alert the imagination of the viewer.

Allow yourself to notice transparent ponds, puddles, windows and curtains to look at deeper regions visible to your eyes. Interior creations are readily discerned and observed. We live in a world of transparent wonders.

Melanie Samson dressed in transparent underwear. She liked to show off as she stood near a long-length mirror to admire her figure. Her transparent undergarments were very revealing. She could pose as a nude model. Melanie wore transparent clothing which revealed her body. She wanted people to notice her.

Cellophane wrappings and tin plastic wrappings are covered over bread, processed foods, frozen foods and pastries. These transparent coverings are clearly seen through.

Maurine Hamilton was an Interior Decorator. She liked to experiment with transparent curtains and objects while she decorated homes, offices and apartments. See-through effects added to the décor in these dwellings. Glass figurines were artistic and attractive. Transparent curtains were draped around bed canopies and different areas around the houses and apartments.

Jeffrey MacIntosh was an architect. He created architectural designs. He illustrated transparent walls and sections to rooms and ceilings. He designed transparent balconies so people could see vivid views clearly. Jeffrey was a very creative and innovative architect.

The world of transparent fibers and textures create an illusion of sheer beauty. Transparency exists in many dimensions and levels of existence for us to become aware of.

FOURTEEN

Microscopes Are Valuable

Microscopes are very valuable. Microscopes are used in science laboratories and medical laboratories. Tiny microbes, bacteria and cells can be seen with a microscope. Biologists are able to see tiny bacteria cells and amoebas under the microscope.

A microscope is an instrument consisting essentially of a lens or combination of lenses, for making very small objects as microorganisms, look larger so that they can be seen and studied according to WEBSTER'S NEW WORD DICTIONARY.

Luis Pasteur discovered how to cure smallpox. He studied smallpox bacteria under the microscope. Cancer cells and DNA strands have been studied with the use of microscopes. Leukemia has been carefully studied by examining blood cells with the use of microscopes. Skin cells and plant cells have been examined with microscopes. Biologists study a variety of leaves and stems under the microscope.

Microscopes have been very valuable to use in order to study microscopic substances. Microbes in a water drop can be examined with the lens of a microscope. Without the use of microscopes, tiny microbes and minute cells would not be seen. Even germs can be observed with the use of microscopes.

FIFTEEN

Herman's Telescope

Herman Stillman was a boy genius. At an early age he became interested in studying the stars and constellation patterns in the night sky. His parents observed Herman's advanced awareness for his age.

Herman continued to study how the stars were located in the sky. He noticed Venus, Mars and Jupiter moving much more quickly in the sky. Herman's parents decided to purchase a telescope for their precocious son.

Herman was excited about his new telescope. At night he stood outside in the backyard to look into his telescope at the night sky. He could see the surface of the Moon. He observed deep, dark craters on the Moon. Herman could observe Venus, Mars and Jupiter much more closely. He was very intrigued with the different colors on these planets. He saw a pink cloudy color on Venus. Mars appeared red. Jupiter had streaks and wavy designs. Jupiter has a huge, moving, swirling red spot that astronomers believe is an immense hurricane.

Herman used his new telescope on clear nights to observe the heavens. He discovered new celestial patterns. He was excited to locate Saturn, Neptune and eventually Uranus. He noticed rings around Jupiter, Saturn and Neptune. Herman was fascinated with his findings.

After observing the night sky night after night, Herman began drawing the constellations and movements of the planets in our solar system. Any new observations were drawn and kept in large folders. Herman kept track of each drawing. He learned by drawing the solar system and constellations.

Herman became very accurate when he drew different drawings of the heavens. He decided he would study Astronomy when he went to college. He was an excellent student throughout elementary and high school. He excelled in Science, Mathematics and many more subjects. He won honors in school and graduated at the top of his high school class.

Herman enjoyed using his telescope for years to study outer space. He noticed different constellation patterns not shown in Astronomy books. He drew these new constellations. He received a B.S, M.S. and Ph.D in Astronomy from a well known university in California near Pasadena.

There is a large planetarium in Pasadena which Herman Stillman went to frequently to observe outer space through a very large telescope. He learned considerably more about the solar system and our galaxy and the

Universe. He developed scientific theories about our galaxy. He found out that there are many solar systems and galaxies. He used computers to visualize outer space. Different galaxies appeared which have millions of solar systems and stars. Herman was amazed how enormous our Cosmos is.

Herman associated with other astronomers. He discussed theories about outer space with them. In time, he wrote an astronomy book entitled NEW THEORIES ABOUT THE COSMOS. His book became well known. He was interviewed by other astronomers in films and videos. Herman Stillman became famous as an astronomer.

Fiction

SIXTEEN

Traveling With A Trailer

Traveling with a trailer is an exciting way to journey across the country. A trailer can be attached to a pickup truck. You can travel to many places and stay in your trailer along the way. You can cook meals, take a shower and sleep in a bed overnight in your trailer.

Trailers can be parked in trailer parks, on campgrounds, on the beach, in driveways and parking lots. Trailers are different sizes from small to very large in length. Travelers can be flexible while they go on vacations.

Vacationers may want to travel to lakes, through verdant-green valleys and up mountainsides as well as travel along the coast near an azure blue ocean. They usually stock up with food and supplies which are kept in their trailers.

Mary and Todd Martinel decided to take a vacation. They packed their 30 foot trailer before they departed on their vacation. They were planning to journey to the Grand Canyon in Arizona. Once the trailer was packed with food and supplies the Martinels hooked their pick up truck to their trailer.

Mary and Todd left at 8:15 a.m. on Saturday morning in mid June. The weather was pleasant. They began their journey from Ukiah, California. Todd drove the truck which was hitched to the long trailer. He stopped at a gas station to fill his truck with gasoline. He checked the four tires on his truck to be sure there was enough air in each tire. He also checked the oil. Then he washed the truck windows while Mary waited in the truck.

The Martinels began their trip after leaving the Ukiah gas station. Todd was able to get on the main highway south. He had a map which he used to study the highway routes. He continued past Lakeport to Clear Lake. The lake was very blue and calm. They stopped and enjoyed the view of this beautiful lake. Mary and Todd observed the surrounding California countryside as they continued to travel on the main road. They observed pine trees clustered near the road. Wild flowers and golden fields of dry grass could be seen for many miles. Oak trees were spread out in the fields and meadows further on.

Todd stopped in Sacramento, California near a Mexican restaurant. He parked the truck with his trailer in a parking area near the restaurant. It was sunny and very warm in Sacramento. Mary and Todd stepped into the Mexican restaurant. They listened to Mexican music. A waitress came to their table with menus. After studying the menus carefully Mary ordered two cheese enchiladas with beans and rice. Todd ordered a large bean and rice burrito with lettuce and tomatoes on the side. Both of them ordered ice tea to cool off. It was 105 degrees outside.

The Mexican restaurant was decorated with serapes and Mexican hats, Mexican dolls and other displays. Paintings of Mexico were hanging on the wall. The server, dressed in a Mexican blouse and skirt, brought the two orders to the table. Mary and Todd began eating their Mexican lunch. They looked around the restaurant to enjoy the Mexican atmosphere as they ate.

After lunch, Mary and Todd went back to their truck hitched to their trailer. Todd continued to drive towards Calaveras and then to Merced. It still was quite warm. They continued on to Fresno, which is a large city. Mary and Todd glanced at avocado groves, apricot groves and many fruit stands near the sides of the road as they traveled inland. When they approached Sequoia National Park, Mary and Todd saw tall, sturdy, sequoia, redwood trees in thick forests.

Sequoia National Park was an ideal place to stay. Todd drove the truck with their trailer into the national park. The sequoia, redwood trees were majestic and fragrant. Mary and Todd parked at a camping spot after paying camping fees at the entrance of this national park. After settling in at the campsite, Mary and Todd relaxed outside as they sat in outdoor chairs. They took deep breaths to absorb the fresh air.

Then Todd took firewood out of the trailer and prepared a campfire. Mary took steaks, raw potatoes, raw carrots, celery and string beans from the trailer refrigerator. Mary prepared the steaks with salt, pepper and some herbs which she sprinkled on the meat and rubbed into it. She began frying the steaks in canola oil. While the steaks were cooking she chopped up potatoes, carrots, celery and string beans which she stir-fried in another pan together with herbs such as basil and oregano. When the meat, potatoes and vegetables were completely stir fried, Mary placed a large cooked steak in each serving dish. She added the cooked vegetables and potatoes to the plates.

It was time to eat. Mary buttered seven grain bread and placed it on the campground table. She also set the table. She poured lemonade into two glasses. Todd came to the table. He had gone into the trailer earlier to take a shower to cool off. Dinner smelled delicious. Mary and Todd sat down to enjoy their evening meal. Todd had been driving many hours to get to Sequoia National Park. Now he could relax and enjoy his meal.

Mary and Todd listened to birds in the sequoia tree forest. The birds chirped a variety of melodic tones. Some birds flew by so Mary and Todd could observe them. It was beginning to get dark outside. After dinner, Mary and Todd cleaned up the campsite. They sat by the open fire for awhile as it cooled off in the evening so they could enjoy the warmth of the fire.

The sequoia trees were quite tall and majestic. Mary and Todd looked up to the top of these ancient trees with awe and wonder. They wondered how old these magnificent trees were. Then at about 9:30 p.m. Mary and Todd stepped into their trailer after putting the campfire out.

That night they slept soundly in their comfortable beds in their trailer. It was quiet in the Sequoia National Park at night. Bears had roamed through this spacious park many years ago. However, Mary and Todd did not notice any bears moving about while they were camping there.

The next morning Mary prepared breakfast for Todd and herself. They ate scrambled eggs, toasted bread and hash browns. Mary prepared coffee to pep them up before they began to travel again. Before they continued their journey towards the Grand Canyon they walked through the sequoia, redwood trees for several hours to appreciate the beauty of these spectacular trees. Then they got into their truck with their trailer attached and headed out of the Sequoia National Park towards Death Valley. It took several hours to reach Death Valley. It was extremely hot, arid climate and dry landscape. It took them at least three hours to pass through Death Valley.

In the mid afternoon Mary and Todd crossed Death Valley. They drove across the Nevada border into Boulder City. They stopped to put gasoline in their truck. They had their truck tires checked. Then they continued to Lake Mead National Recreation Area. They parked their truck and trailer.

Mary and Todd stayed several days and nights at Lake Mead. They went fishing for freshwater trout and mackerel after they rented a rowboat into the middle of the deep blue lake. The water was very cold. Todd and

Mary put fish bait on the hooks of their strings to their fishing poles. They threw the baited hooks into the lake and they waited for fish to bite. They enjoyed looking across the lake at the azure blue water. They observed ripples and some flying fish. Finally, fish began biting the baited hooks. Todd pulled a big trout out of the lake into the rowboat. Mary also caught a fish and pulled it in near the boat. She struggled to pull a mackerel into the boat. Todd helped Mary get the fish into the boat.

Todd and Mary rowed back to shore. They walked back to their trailer. Mary washed the fish. She wrapped the mackerel up and put it in the freezer in the trailer. Then she cut up the trout and fried it in canola oil. She salted the trout as it was cooking. She boiled potatoes. While the potatoes were cooking Mary prepared a green salad with dark green lettuce, shredded carrots, cut green pepper, baby tomatoes, cucumbers and onions. She prepared a salad dressing with olive oil, herbs, salt and pepper. She poured the salad dressing in the salad and tossed the salad with the dressing. When the potatoes were boiled Mary took them out of the pan. She placed the boiled potatoes in a bowl and mashed them thoroughly. She added salt and butter into the mashed potatoes.

Mary and Todd sat outside at a table and ate the trout, mashed potatoes and green salad. They ate slices of seven grain bread with their meal. They sipped ice tea with their meal. For dessert they ate sliced, raw peaches and strawberries. After dinner, they sat near their trailer and gazed at the stars in the night sky. The night air was cooler. Mary and Todd slept in their trailer again that night.

The next day Mary and Todd went swimming in Lake Mead. They splashed around in the cold water. Then they came out of the lake and rested on the grass near the lake in the sun. The warmth of the sun made them feel better. They walked along the edge of the lake to enjoy the marvelous view. Later, they ate at a restaurant near the lake. There was a wonderful window view from the restaurant. Mary ordered salmon with wild rice and mixed vegetables. She sipped clam chowder before the main course. Todd ordered halibut with wild rice. He had a salad with lettuce, tomatoes and cucumbers. He selected Italian dressing to put on his salad. Mary and Todd enjoyed custard pudding with whipped cream for dessert. They sipped white wine after dinner.

The next day Todd and Mary headed towards the Grand Canyon. Todd drove north into Colorado to Arizona. He drove for several hours until Mary and he had reached the most spectacular canyon in the world. The Grand Canyon in Arizona was very immense and spectacular to view. Mary and Todd stepped out of their truck to appreciate the scenic view of this magnificent canyon. They observed layered, red sediment along the ridges of the canyon walls. The Grand Canyon was very deep with the Colorado River flowing through it.

Todd and Mary parked their trailer in a camping area near the canyon. They went riding on mules in the Grand Canyon with a group of people who also rode mules. They observed the canyon interior closely as they rode their mules. They saw squirrels, chipmunks and Blue Jays moving around in scrubs, dry grass and behind rocks. They noticed deer roaming in the canyon. The deer were nibbling leaves and grass. They pranced away quickly when the mule riders came into sight. There were no bears in the canyon.

Mary and Todd continued riding mules in the canyon all day. The temperature changed during the day. It was hot and then it was colder. They took off their jackets when it was warm. Then they wore their jackets when it was colder. Mary and Todd stayed at the Grand Canyon several days. They went in a large rubber raft down the Colorado River. The river rapids were very swift. The raft floated down the river against rough currents and down large rapids and small waterfalls.

Mary and Todd experienced sudden dangers while they were in the rubber raft. The raft nearly crashed into some rocks in the Colorado River. Then the raft almost turned over in the rougher rapids. Mary and Todd felt the turbulent water causing the raft to flip up in the air. They held on for dear life. They thought they were goners. Somehow, the raft didn't flip over far enough to capsize. Mary and Todd survived and they were saved from drowning in the river.

Todd and Mary returned to their truck and trailer. It was time to travel back to Ukiah in California where they resided. On the way back they thought about the wonderful times they had on this vacation. The biggest highlight was their mule ride through the Grand Canyon. They recalled the majestic, sequoia, redwood trees at the Sequoia National Park as well. They had taken photographs of their adventures traveling from Ukiah, California to the Grand Canyon in Arizona and back to Ukiah, California. They put many photographs of their journey in a photo album so they could enjoy looking at photos of their marvelous vacation.

Fiction

SEVENTEEN

The Skater

Jeanette Spaulding became interested in roller skating when she was seven years old. She often went to a skating rink in Baltimore, Maryland where she lived to watch different skaters gliding and moving swiftly around the skating rink.

Jeanette began learning to skate with the assistance of her older brother, Ben, who was a good skater. Ben was fourteen years old. He held Jeanette's hand and helped her skate around the skating rink. Jeanette was glad to receive her brother's assistance so she could learn to skate.

As Jeanette practiced skating on a regular basis she continued to skate better and better. She learned to twirl in a circular motion, to spin and jump in the air and land gracefully. Jeanette also learned to dance with partners as she skated around the skating rink.

Jeanette became a very good roller skater. She purchased beautiful skating outfits to wear to the skating rink. She decided to become a professional skater. She tried out for skating contests. She attended every contest she found out about. Friday evening on April 7th, 2009 Jeanette entered her first major skating contest at age 14. She was dressed in a sparkling pink, skating outfit with a short skirt and attractive blouse. Jeanette looked very attractive in her new skating outfit.

There was a large audience in the skating rink in the bleachers ready to enjoy the skating contest. Twelve skating contestants assembled to compete for a first place gold cup and $250 prize. Second place would receive a special ribbon and $50.

Jeanette was last to perform in the roller skating contest. She waited in the bleachers near the other skating contestants. She was nervous while she waited. She observed each contestant perform. All of the contestants wore attractive, skating outfits. The audience clapped loudly for most of the contestants. Jeanette finally was called to perform. A classical piece was played from a record while Jeanette performed. She began her performance and moved across the skating rink carefully. She maintained her performance movements. She made several swift swirls and then she jumped in the air and came down without falling onto the smooth, wooden floor. She continued to move gracefully around the skating rink. Jeanette glided around and turned around in different directions making creative movements.

When Jeanette had completed her performance the audience clapped very loudly. Jeanette bowed gracefully several times. Then she went back to her seat with the other performers. She waited to find out who had won the roller skating contest. She hoped to be one of the winners. Finally, the judges cheered for Jeanette.

Jeanette thanked the judge. Tears came down her cheeks because she was overjoyed because she had won first place at the age of fourteen. She had her skating career ahead of her. Jeanette looked forward to entering in more roller skating contests to continue competing so she would become well known for her skating performances. She wanted to become the best roller skater in the world.

EIGHTEEN

Raptures At Ebb Tide

Raptures at ebb tide console us emotionally. The back and forth rhythm of the ocean tides causes us to feel the rhythmic balance of ocean waves.

Walking near the ocean is relaxing as the tide moves across our feet and legs. Crabs and shellfish are washed ashore. The wet beach sand is smooth to walk on. The wet sand is usually cooler than the dry, hot, beach sand.

Listen carefully to the sound of waves moving in the ocean. The rhythmic sounds of splashing waves echo for miles. Crashing waves have a special sound. You can enjoy the spectacular view of the vast ocean.

Look at the horizon in the distance where the sun sets every night. Light reflects on the ocean and wet sand near the shore. The ebb tide continues to and fro every 24 hours. The flowing movement of the ocean continues day and night. Currents in the ocean move across the ocean with sudden rip tides and white caps.

The sand on the beaches comes from soil and rocks which erode and move toward the ocean shores. Wind, rain and splashing water break down the hard rocks into particles of sand. The black sands in Hawaii come from eroded, black lava to create a black sand beach. Waves splash back and forth along the shore.

Feel the rhythm of the pulsating ocean on the pounding shores on your bare feet. The ebb tide motion will relax you as you walk along the shore near the edge of the ocean. Each time you walk on the beach observe the to and fro motion of the ocean. The Moon affects the ocean currents. Observe rippling waves splashing to the shore.

NINETEEN

Shelley's Baby

Shelley Williams was an attractive, young woman of 22 years old. She often dated men when they asked her out. She responded to their affection and caresses. She was not aware of how to prevent getting pregnant. She continued to become intimate with different men.

One day Shelley no longer had a menstrual period. Four months went by and Shelly began to worry if she was pregnant. She decided to go see a doctor, who examined her carefully. The doctor told Shelley that she was four months pregnant.

Shelley went home and kept her pregnancy a secret from her parents and friends. As time went by Shelley gained weight. She appeared pregnant in her fourth month. Her abdomen expanded out. Her parents noticed that Shelley was gaining weight. Shelley hesitated to tell her mother why she was gaining weight. Shelley's mother, Nora Williams, looked worried. She suspected that Shelley was pregnant because her abdomen had enlarged while Shelley hadn't gained weight in other parts of her body.

Shelley tried to change the subject. She told her mother that she was feeling fine. Then Shelley said she was looking for a job downtown. Nora Williams sensed that Shelley was dodging the issue about gaining weight. So, Shelley's mother decided to talk about something else. Shelley was relieved that her mother was willing to change the subject.

Shelley said, "I have been going to job interviews to get a computer processing job." Nora Williams asked, "Have you been accepted for a job position yet?" Shelley answered, "So far I haven't been able to get a job. I am competing with other job applicants. It is difficult to get a good job. I have submitted my resume to over 20 places .No one has contacted me." Nora Williams looked concerned. She knew jobs were hard to get. Fortunately, Shelley was able to live with her parents. She didn't have to pay rent or utilities. Her parents also provided meals for their daughter.

Shelley's father, David Williams, was employed as an engineer. Nora Williams, his wife, had a part time job as a receptionist at a business firm downtown. She worked in the mornings from 8 a.m. to 12 noon. She came home after her morning job to prepare lunch. She seldom ate out in order to save money on food. Shelley ate lunch with her mother. Shelley's father came home at 5:30 p.m. Shelley and her parents ate dinner together usually at 6 p.m.

That night when David Williams came home at approximately 5:30 p.m. Shelley's mother had prepared roast chicken, wild rice, a medley of steamed vegetables, homemade, whole grain bread, custard pudding and iced her tea for the evening meal. David Williams was called to the dinner table at approximately 6:00 p.m.

Nora Williams and Shelley had placed the evening dinner on the table. The dining room table had been set before dinner by Shelley. Nora Williams had selected flowers from the garden to display on the dining room table. When Nora, David and Shelley were seated at the dining room table, Nora said a prayer before the family began eating their dinner. The platter of roast chicken, wild rice, vegetables and bread were passed around the table. Each one served his or her own food at the table. The Williams began eating.

David Williams was quiet at first at the dining room table. Nora Williams spoke first. She said, "I will have a new boss very soon at my job because Mr. Hoffman is retiring next week. Mr. Hoffman started the business firm thirty years ago. I guess he wants to retire so he can travel around the world. He must be at least 65 or 67 by now." David looked at Nora and replied, "It is nice that he can retire. Now he will have time to do what he wants. I have 20 years to go. I sure would like to travel around the world."

Shelley was listening intently to her parents. She sat quietly. Then her father looked at her. He asked, "What did you do today Shelley?" Shelley smiled at her father and responded. "I helped Mom in the garden and we cooked dinner together." David Williams noticed Shelley's abdomen had expanded considerably. He decided not to comment about Shelley's physical condition. Yet, he felt concerned about her weight gain. He asked, "Have you heard about any job positions yet?" Shelley responded, "I've been trying to get a job. No one has called me to offer a job yet." Shelley went on eating her dinner.

After dinner, Shelley cleaned up the dining room table and she took the dinner dishes, platters and silverware to the kitchen. Then she washed the dishes, dried them and put the dried plates, silverware and platters away in the kitchen cupboards and drawers. Shelley went into her bedroom to be by herself. She decided to lay on her bed and read a book she had bought in a bookstore downtown. She thought about her predicament.

It was too late for Shelley to get an abortion. Besides, she did not believe in abortion. To take the life of a living fetus was very wrong to do. Shelley planned to go to full term with the pregnancy. She would have to accept the consequences of having her baby. She wondered if her baby would be a girl or a boy.

Shelley continued to look for a job downtown. Unfortunately, she was not contacted for a job position. Shelley kept a cell phone with her in case anyone called to offer her a job. Meanwhile, she kept busy helping her mother around the house and in the garden. She hoped she would be able to become independent someday if she became employed. She would have to wait for that day.

Months went by and Shelley was getting closer and closer to delivery of her baby. She finally had the courage to tell her parents that she was pregnant. Her father was deeply concerned that Shelley didn't know who the father was of his daughter's baby. Shelley's mother was glad Shelley had finally revealed that she was going to have a baby.

There was an extra bedroom in Shelley's parents' home. Shelley prepared a nursery in the spare room. She purchased a used crib, dressers, baby clothes, toys, diapers, baby bottles and other necessary items for her baby with her mother's help and financial assistance. The nursery was nicely decorated with a cheerful décor.

As Shelley approached the day or night of the delivery she exercised to prepare for this event. In May she was to have her baby delivered around the seventh of the month. Shelley felt her baby kicking inside of her. She wasn't able to sleep well for several months before the baby was born. She didn't confront any of the men she had sex with because she wasn't sure who the father was.

The awaited day finally arrived. Shelley began feeling sharp labor pains. Then her water bag broke. It was time to go to the nearby hospital so that she could have her baby delivered. Her parents took Shelley to the emergency room at the hospital. Shelley was examined and taken to the delivery room which was the operating room. A doctor at the hospital, who was Doctor Ryan Mitchell, was on call to deliver Shelley's baby. Shelley was placed on the delivery bed. She was given anesthesia to lessen the pain before and during delivery.

Shelley's parents waited in the waiting room while Shelley was having her baby. They hoped she would have a successful delivery. Her parents wished their daughter knew who the father was. They were quite understanding when she told them that she was pregnant. She was lucky to have such good parents, who cared about her and her circumstances.

While Shelley was in the delivery room she tried to cooperate with the doctor and nurses. She was kept awake throughout the delivery. She felt a lot of pain and pressure. She didn't need a C-Section delivery. She was expected to push over and over until the baby came out. Shelley was asked to breathe deeply and then continue to push until her baby came out. Finally, Shelley's baby came out of her womb. It was red. The doctor cut the umbilical cord and tied it. The baby was spanked on its behind so it would start breathing.

Shelley's baby was a boy. He was washed carefully and put into a warm blanket to keep it warm. Meanwhile, the doctor cleaned Shelley up. She was finally numbed. A few stitches were taken where the skin had torn. Shelley was exhausted from the delivery. However, she wanted to see her newborn baby. A nurse brought Shelley's baby to her bedside.

Shelley held here baby boy. He looked healthy and all his fingers and toes were there. He had blue eyes and he weighed eight pounds, 6 ounces. He was a beautiful baby. Shelley's baby was taken to the baby nursery and kept in a baby bed.

Shelley's parents were told that Shelley's baby was born. They were allowed to go to a window at the baby nursery to look at the baby. This was their first grandchild. They looked at the baby and were pleased it looked healthy. They were glad Shelley's delivery was successful.

When Shelley had rested for awhile, her parents were allowed to come into her hospital room to see her. They greeted their daughter warmly. Nora Williams spoke, "Your baby is beautiful Shelley. We were told he is a boy." Shelley smiled at her mother. She was still recuperating from the delivery. She said, "I'm glad the delivery is over! It was painful to deliver. My baby looked good when the nurse showed him to me."

Shelley's father said, "We are proud of you Shelley. Have you thought of a name for your son?" Shelley paused and then said, "I think I will call him Aaron. What do you think of that name?" Nora responded, "That is a good name. We know you need to rest now. We will come back soon." Shelley's parents left Shelley's hospital room. They went home.

Shelley rested overnight in the hospital. Her baby was brought to her regularly, so she could nurse her son and give him attention and become acquainted with him. She was pleased that her baby son responded well and that he was healthy. She planned to remain single while she raised him. She would raise her son in her parents' home until she was strong enough and was working and able to support herself someday. Presently, there was no hurry. Her parents were willing to accept Shelley's baby in their home. Shelley was better off living at her parents' home at the present time.

TWENTY

The Nearby Pond

A nearby pond existed in the countryside near a meadow. The pond was blue when the sky was blue. The pond changed colors as the sky was covered with clouds or fog. Life was teaming in this pond.

Frogs dwelled in the pond. They croaked often as they hopped about looking for food. Frogs used their tongues to grab insects which they swallowed whole because they have no teeth. Frogs sit on lily pads to sun themselves and to rest. They may fall asleep while they are resting. The pond provides a place to receive a lot of moisture and water. Frogs swim around using their legs to move about in the water. Frogs keep their bodies wet to remain healthy. They eat gnats, mosquitoes and small insects which fly by and fly near the frogs.

Frogs are tadpoles when they are babies. They eventually grow into frogs and continue to grow into bigger frogs. Many frogs dwell at the pond croaking in unison.

Lily pods grow abundantly in the pond. Lily pods spread across the pond and provide an array of green designs and places for insects to land to rest and eat as well as to experience the sun's light and heat. Even if insects are cold blooded they benefit from the sun. Dragonflies, mosquitoes and gnats fly in swarms to the pond to receive water and food.

The pond provides water and food for a variety of birds such as ducks, robins, blue jays, swallows, meadowlarks and many more birds. The pond is like an oasis for meadow life that depended on water to survive. Birds land on the lily pods to sun themselves and to drink water. They search for bugs and algae in the pond.

The pond provides a place for carp and gold fish to live. Ponds exist at resorts, public gardens and in gardens at individual homes. Ponds add beauty to any environment. Many creatures, water plants, fish, insects and birds depend on healthy ponds to thrive and to continue to exist.

TWENTY-ONE

The Shoe Factory

Shoe factories produce a variety of shoes for the public. Shoes are carefully manufactured step by step and boxed to be sent to many shoe stores. We need to wear shoes to protect our feet.

Joseph Goodman grew up in Toledo, Ohio. His father produced shoes in a shoe factory. Joseph often went to his father's shoe factory in the section of this city where factories existed. Joseph observed how different leather and cloth shoes are made. He became interested in making shoes.

When Joseph had free time he experimented with shoe patterns. He learned to cut leather parts such as the frame of a shoe, a tongue and to make shoe heels. He learned to make hand made shoes with buckled and shiny leather which he created so that the shoes he made would look attractive. He stretched out each pair of shoes with a shoe stretcher so they would be comfortable and durable.

As Joseph got older he graduated from high school. He decided to take after his father to become a shoe maker. He began working part time at his father's shoe factory when he was sixteen. When he became eighteen and completed high school he began working at the shoe factory full time.

Joseph had begun working with a minimum wage. After he worked at the shoe factory five years, his father increased Joseph's wages. His father hoped his son would continue to work at his shoe factory. He hoped Joseph would one day take over the shoe factory when he retired. Joseph continued to work at his father's shoe factory for twenty years.

Joseph had developed innovative ideas in making creative and very different shoes. He made open and closed shoes with modern looking colors. He experimented with different textures and colors so that he created very attractive, new shoes.

Joseph showed his father the new shoes he had created. He told his father that these new shoes could become popular and would be purchased by many people. Joseph's father, Timothy Goodman looked at his son with a concerned expression. He replied, "I think these shoes look unusual. However, we only make conventional shoes with leather and thick cloth fiber. Our factory shoes have been sold across the country. I don't want to spend any more than I have been spending for the factory shoes we are already producing and selling to shoe companies.

Timothy Goodman continued to have a concerned, serious expression on his face. He noticed his son's disappointed expression. Joseph responded, "These new shoes may bring in a lot more money. We can make a difference in the shoe industry by making these new shoes." Joseph's father answered, "I don't want to risk making your new shoes at this time."

Joseph knew his father was stubborn about making changes at the shoe factory. He would have to abide by his father's wishes. Joseph was twenty years old. He could wait until he inherited his father's shoe factory someday. Joseph continued to help produce conventional shoes for many years to come. He would have to be patient.

When Joseph was forty years old his father was 67 years old. His father decided to retire. Joseph was asked to become the manager of his father's shoe factory. Joseph was in charge now. He was able to make his own decisions at the shoe factory. He decided to produce his new shoe designs and he would sell these new shoes to different shoe stores around the country. He began making the new shoes with different textures and fibers. He colored the new shoes with bright, cheerful colors. His new shoes looked glamorous and unconventional.

Joseph sent his new shoes to many shoe stores. Customers tried on these new, colorful shoes. Many customers purchased the new shoes. Millions of the new, glamorous shoes were sold across the country. Joseph made millions of dollars because his new shoes were very popular. Different age groups enjoyed wearing and displaying these new, modern shoes.

Once Joseph received millions of dollars he expanded his shoe making business. He had new shoe factories built in major cities in America. His new shoes became well known. He had succeeded in trying his innovative, new shoe designs.

Nonfiction

TWENTY-TWO

The Artist's Studio

Artists usually have a studio to keep their art supplies and artistic achievements such as paintings, sculptures, pottery and other artistic achievements. They keep oil and watercolor paints, sculpture stones and clay in their studios. Art paper and canvases are stored in their studios.

Well known artists generally have larger studios. They have more money because their art work has been sold to many buyers who appreciate their artistic endeavors. Artists who are not well known generally have much smaller studios.

Artists move about to paint different scenes outdoors in valleys, meadows, near the ocean and near mountainsides, etc. Some artists draw portraits of people at County Fairs, at art festivals and at areas where art work is displayed. Artists display their art work on stands near the harbor, in parks and art galleries.

An artist usually keeps his or her studio organized and neat. An artist is able to find art supplies such as paint brushes, paints, art canvasses in cupboards in his or her studio. The artist continues to supply himself or herself with more art supplies in order to go on creating new artistic achievements.

Some artists teach aspiring students how to paint, make sculptures and make pottery, etc in their art studios. Well established artists usually have a lot of students, who learn how to become accomplished artists over a period of time. Artists continue to collect student art work to display in art galleries.

TWENTY-THREE

Metaphysics Will Enlighten You

Metaphysics is the study of ancient eastern and western wisdom religions. The spiritual laws are of love, unity, reincarnation, polarities, magnetism, centralization, attraction and repulsion, cause and effect known as karma and balance and equilibrium.

Metaphysics means to go beyond the physical plane into the inner planes which are invisible to the physical eyes. Metaphysics helps us understand universal laws and spiritual realities. There are seven planes of existence to become consciously aware of. We need to realize that we operate and exist on seven planes. The physical plane is one of the seven planes. Six planes are invisible. Yet they interconnect within us.

Students of Metaphysics are able to broaden their awareness of cosmic consciousness. They can become more enlightened about the supreme intelligence of God. Angels, archangels, elohim and ascended Masters serve in the Great White Brotherhood within the White Lodge. They are willing to serve humanity.

Metaphysical students can learn to understand the four elements of fire, air, water and earth. Higher elementals serve the Earth kingdoms of nature. Fire, air, water and earth elements exist in our human bodies and in the animal and plant kingdoms. These four elements are necessary in order for life to exist on Earth. The four elements of fire, air, water and earth need to be balanced on Earth in order to help living things to grow and thrive.

The law of cycles also exists. There are cycles of time which affect humanity and the Earth. Each cycle gives us the opportunity to evolve and awaken to God's divine plan. We have the opportunity to realize the Cosmic Plan of God from lifetime to lifetime as we reincarnate. The cosmic clock keeps ticking. Time exists especially on the physical plane. On inner planes time becomes timeless. Celestial beings exist in these inner dimensions. They move about freely within inner space.

Metaphysics has been a spiritual science on Earth since very ancient, times in Lemuria, Atlantis, Sumeria, Babylon, Asia, Europe and America. Ancient sages and avatars have been aware of metaphysical truths. The Theosophical Society began in 1875 when Madame Helena Blavatksy established this New Age Movement. She introduced reincarnation and karma known as cause and effect. She wrote THE SECRET DOCTRINE, ISIS UNVEILED, KEYS TO THEOSOPHY and questionnaire pamphlets about Metaphysics.

Other metaphysical students such as Francia La Due, William Quan Judge, William David Dower, Rudolph Steiner, Max Hendell, Godfrey Ray King, Alice Bailey and Annie Besant continued to write metaphysical books to enlighten humanity.

The Temple Of The People was founded in 1898 in Syracuse, New York in America. This metaphysical movement came to Halcyon, California in 1903. The Temple Of The People has existed for 112 years on the physical plane. Universal laws, principles and concepts have been written about in Temple metaphysical books such as THE TEMPLE TEACHINGS, Volumes I, II and III, THE MOUNTAINTOP, Volumes I, II and III, PORTFOLIO MESSAGES and THE TEMPLE ARTISANS. These valuable, metaphysical writings are very worthwhile to study. You can become very enlightened if your become aware of Metaphysics.

TWENTY-FOUR

Cats Have Unusual Perception

Cats have unusual perception. They have excellent, night vision. Cats are capable of hearing sounds far away as well as very high frequency sounds which human beings are unable to hear.

Cats have extrasensory perception. They are able to see auras and astral images. They use their tails to sense vibrations. They are quick to see people and animals coming towards them.

Cats purr when they are relaxed and given affectionate attention by different people. They enjoy being petted. They like to scratch furniture with their claws. Their eyes and ears inform cats of harmful conditions.

When cats see auras of people they are psychic. They perceive emotional swings in people such as fear, anger, anxiety as well as peace. They detect how people react by listening to their voices and observing their facial expressions.

Cats can travel for many miles and then find their way back to the locations they started from. They sleep near houses, in gardens and barns. Because of their night vision they are able to walk at night for miles in the dark.

Cats are able to spot gophers, mice and other rodents readily in the ground. They hear gophers under the ground. They also observe birds nearby. Cats chase after rodents and birds to eat.

Cats are independent pets. They come and go. They like to rest and sun themselves in sunny and shady places outdoors. They may walk up to you and rub against your legs. They move their tails back and forth when they want to communicate.

TWENTY-FIVE

Concentric Rings

Concentric rings are rings within rings. Circles within circles exist. If you throw a rock in a pool you will see circular ripples spreading out from the center where the rock was thrown in the pool.

Concentric rings make interesting designs for book covers, bulletin boards and posters. Rings or circles become larger and larger when they are concentric circles. Rings or circles start from the center. You can make alternate colors which blend in harmony.

Concentric circles are geometric designs which are interesting to observe. Artists are able to create concentric rings on canvas and they can paint bright colors on the concentric rings. Concentric rings can look magnificent.

Massive, concentric rings stand out even from a distance. They may have an unusual look to viewers. Artists have experimented with concentric rings. Tiny, concentric rings even create an artistic, geometric effect on viewers.

The biggest example of concentric rings in our solar system are the rings of Saturn that are thousands of miles wide. Narrower rings surround Jupiter and Uranus.

The capital city of Atlantis was called Poseid, and according to Plato it consisted of concentric rings. The city was built in circles of paved roads and canals. Other roads radiated out from the circular center like spokes in a wheel.

Some of the mysterious crop circles contain concentric circles with geometrical patterns.

TWENTY-SIX

Different Kinds Of Energy

There are many kinds of energy in the world. Electrical energy exists in nature. Humanity has learned to harness electrical energy. Electricity is used in buildings, homes, street lights and home appliances such as ovens, refrigerators, microwave ovens, toasters, irons, water heaters, tools and cars. Boats are operated with electric engines or motors.

Lightning creates electricity. Electrical energy exists in lightning. Electricity can be generated in water. Electricity is generated around the world. Millions of people depend on electricity in their homes for lighting, cooking, preservation of food and is used in many home appliances.

Conduction of electricity or transmission of heat and the passage of energy from particle to particle is a form of conductivity. Conductors are substances that conduct electricity.

Water creates H20 and produces energy. Cold water has cold energy. Warmer water produces heat. Heat is a form of energy. Gas produces heat energy used in stove and water heaters and in regular heaters.

Wood can be burned to create heat. Fire is a form of energy which produces heat. Fires cause forests and houses to burn down. Volcanoes produce heat and lava which can change the landscape. Volcanoes even erupt in the depths of the ocean floor.

Coal is burned to produce heat energy. Heat is needed especially when the climate is very cold. Gas heat is used in stoves to cook food. Ovens in stoves also bake different food such as meat, casseroles, cakes, cookies, muffins, bread, brownies, rolls and pies, etc. A certain amount of heat protects humanity on a regular basis. Heat is a form of fire which is energy.

Energy manifests in fire, air, water and earth. Without energy life would not exist. Energy continues to manifest in different forms on Earth.

Oil and gasoline are consumed in vehicles which move for many miles. Trucks, vans, regular cars, RV Campers and motor trailers depend on gasoline and oil to burn in their motors in order for vehicles to move and travel around. Energy is necessary so magnetism can exist. We need energy in our cells in our physical bodies. We depend on fire, air, water and earth elements to function in our human bodies. All of nature's species, plants and water depend on the four elements of fire, air, water and earth to exist. The energy within these elements keeps nature in existence.

TWENTY-SEVEN

Insects Respond

Insects have the sense of sight, touch, smell and taste. Many insects respond to the weather as it changes day by day and at night. Insects are affected by the sun, wind, rain, sleet, fog and mist. Many insects crawl on the ground and live near plants. Some insects live in trees. Insects are cold blooded. Some insects have wings while other insects depend only on legs to walk around. Insects depend on their eyes to look for food. There are species of insects that only eat plants and other species that are carnivorous. . Insects are much smaller than human beings. Some insects are nocturnal while other insects come out only during the day to move around and function.

Grasshoppers are able to fly. They also hop around from plant to plant. They eat leaves on plants. Grasshoppers fly in large groups and swarm around looking for food.

Grasshoppers are green and they have antennas so they can perceive their environment. Grasshoppers are capable of eating up many leaves, wheat crops, barley and other crops as they swarm together to eat. Both grasshoppers and locusts swarm by the thousands to devastate the landscape as they eat up many crops.

Grasshoppers and locusts do not bite human beings. However, if they swarm onto people they can be harmful if they crawl into a person's eyes and ears and female private parts.

Spiders usually hide near rocks. They hide in shady places. Many spiders create webs in bushes, on plants and in trees. Spiders capture insects in their webs. They eat the insects once they are dead. Spiders have more legs than other insects. Some spiders are poisonous while other spiders are harmless and are not poisonous. Spiders help to bring about a balance in nature.

Sal bugs have shells. Snails also have shells. Sal bugs can hide their entire body inside their shells. Snails can hide inside their shells as well. These bugs usually live out their life cycles. They hide under big rocks. They eat mineral substances in soil.

Millions of insects live on the Earth. Ants live in colonies. There are black and red ants. Some ants are very large while other ants are very small. They gather moisture off of leaves and inside soils. Ants usually crawl into dead logs which are hollow. They may live under logs in the shade.

Some ants go into people's houses to look for food and to stay indoors away from the hot sun. Some ants live under houses where it is dark. Ants continue to live in colonies. There is a queen ant that produces ant eggs which eventually hatch. New ants are born and they live in the colonies. Red ants sting people. Black ants don't usually sting people. When it rains ants stay in logs and on large leaves and branches. They move quickly to shelter to avoid drowning. Ants usually live in climates where there is no snow.

Beetles crawl around on the ground. They collect leaves and grass. Some beetles collect waste matter. Beetles are different sizes and colors. They have lived on the Earth for millions of years.

Insects have feelings. They run away from danger. They experience fear as well as group awareness. Insects have the instinct to survive. They have learned to create a place to live. For instance, bees build hives to live in. They gather pollen to produce honey. The honey is kept in wax cones. The queen bee produces eggs which hatch into bees, drones and more queen bees. Bee workers hunt for pollen which they store in the hive. Bee workers do all the work. They build the beehive and look after the queen bee and drones. Bee colonies are very organized. Bee hives are usually built high in trees. Bee workers are obedient and they follow through with their work.

Insects help to promote a balance in nature. Many insects have lived on Earth millions of years. Insects live around the world in many locations and in different climates.

TWENTY EIGHT

Healing Power

Healing power exists. Some people have the ability to heal other people. Laying on of hands is one method of healing. Magnetic energy flows through the healers hands in a person's body. Magnetic energy harmonizes body cells and relieves pain, tension and anxieties.

Healing prayers can help one overcome illnesses and diseases. Decrees can be chanted powerfully to the angels, archangels, higher elementals, elohim and Masters to ask illnesses and sickness to be stopped. Healing prayers can be chanted over and over to help individuals overcome maladies and diseases.

Healing power exists in certain springs which exist in specific places in the world. Lourdes in France has a healing spring. Many people have come to Lourdes to be healed in its spring water. They have been healed by stepping in the healing spring.

People have been cured of arthritis, lumbago, skin cancer, lung congestion, paralysis of the muscles, eye afflictions, rheumatism and many more maladies and diseases. The healing spring cleared these diseases. People went home healed of their afflictions.

The white light of God has healing rays which heal the physical and astral cells so a person can be healed of different illnesses and afflictions. The white light penetrates diseased cells so diseases are dissolved and erased from body cells on the physical and astral planes. Healing power exists and can be used to heal many conditions.

Laser beams are used to remove cataracts from people's eyes. Organs in the human body have been healed without surgery by the laying on of hands. No incisions are made. Yet, a person's diseased organs have been cured.

Faith in God and the use of healing power can make the difference in being healed and restored to better health. We need to pray for physical wellness and Christ wholeness on a regular basis.

A person can be healed by exercising regularly and eating organic foods. Raw, organic vegetables and fruits help to restore your body. Garlic, onions, natural herbs such as cloves, mint, sage, thyme, basil and oregano, etc. help to keep our physical bodies healthier. Healing power exists in sunlight. The sun's rays contain Vitamin D and E especially. We can remain healthy if we live by divine laws and stay close to nature. Deep breaths to oxidize our body cells help to bring about good breathing habits. We are restored to good health by focusing on how to stay healthy.

TWENTY-NINE

Encounters With A Space Being

Maxine Schuler liked to hike around in the dunes near Oceano, California. She lived near the dunes. So, she walked into the dunes which had high mounds of sand which rippled in the wind. Maxine was in her forties. She lived alone.

As Maxine strolled through the dunes one day the warm sun touched her body. The sand was quite warm. Maxine decided to sit down to rest on a high dune. She could see for miles to the horizon at the edge of the ocean. The beach stretched for miles in the distance. Maxine continued to gaze at the spectacular view. She was intrigued with this scenery.

Then Maxine fell asleep with the warm sun blazing on her skin. When she woke up she saw someone standing near her. She was startled when she saw a tall, long blonde haired, blue eyed man dressed in a white and purple robe with gold sandals standing there looking at her.

This stranger appeared friendly and radiant. Maxine suddenly felt white light emanating from this celestial being. She sensed that he was not from the Earth. This celestial being spoke to Maxine. He said, "Don't be alarmed. I come in peace. My name is Julio." Maxine began to calm down. She hadn't expected to meet such an unusual being especially in the dunes. Maxine asked, "Where did you come from?"

Julio replied, "I come from The Pleiades which is billions of light years away." Maxine asked, "Why did you come to Earth?" Julio said, "The Earth is in danger. Large asteroids are heading this way from the asteroid belt between Mars and Jupiter. Maxine stared at Julio with a very concerned expression. She asked, "How do you know about these asteroids?" Julio answered, "I have seen asteroids whirling in space headed this way as I passed by in my spaceship. There are a lot of asteroids floating around. A planet called Maldek exploded between Mars and Jupiter" thousands of years ago. The asteroids are shattered particles from that destroyed planet."

Maxine asked, "How soon will the asteroids come to Earth?" Julio said, "They may be here very soon." Maxine asked, "Can anything be done about the asteroids?" Julio answered, "I will shoot laser beams at them to stop them from crashing to Earth." Maxine, who still had a worried expression on her face, replied, "Will the laser beams be strong enough to destroy these asteroids?" Julio replied, "I believe the laser beams will destroy the asteroids. I have used laser beams many times before to destroy other asteroids. However, the asteroids coming this way are much larger than other asteroids. I will use much stronger laser beams to shatter them."

Maxine realized that Julio was an amazing, celestial being. He appeared to know a lot about asteroids. Maxine asked, "Where is your spaceship?" Julio said, "My spaceship is parked on the dunes farther away. If you look to the east you will be able to see it." Maxine looked to the east along the dunes. She noticed a silver, saucer shaped spaceship in the dunes. She was amazed at the spaceship. There were round windows around the spaceship and the spaceship was also round.

Julio said, "Would you like to come with me to see my spaceship up close?" Maxine hesitated at first to go. Julio continued, "I have something to show you in my spaceship." Maxine decided to walk to Julio's spaceship. They both walked east through the rolling dunes until they came up close to the spaceship. Julio pressed a remote control with his majestic right hand. The door to the spaceship opened suddenly. A platform opened up. Julio encouraged Maxine to walk up the platform into the open doorway into the spaceship.

When Maxine entered the silver, metallic spaceship she saw, a radiant, violet room with counters and modern looking furniture. She was able to look out the round windows. She could see the Earth's environment from these windows. Julio and Maxine continued walking through the lit up room until they came to a panel. He pressed a button and the panel opened up.

Maxine was amazed to see a large screen with motion pictures of another planet which she had never seen before. She saw geometric plants, a violet sky and a rose colored waterway which appeared to be an ocean. The geometric plants were swaying around and some of the plants were moving around. Some plants were gold and some were a bluish color. Maxine saw sparkling stars in the violet sky which dazzled. She was filled with awe and wonder about what she saw on the screen.

Julio smiled at Maxine and said, "The beings on my planet live in peace. We live without wars. We have central leadership on our planet. We have an excellent climate because we are able to balance nature." Maxine asked, "What is the name of your planet?" Julio replied, "My planet is called Clarion". Maxine responded, "That is a beautiful name."

Maxine noticed computers and digital equipment on different counters and tables. Julio offered Maxine an ambrosia drink. She decided to try it. Julio poured a purple juice mixture into a crystal glass and he handed the ambrosia drink to Maxine. She sipped this drink very slowly. It tasted like a mixture of grape and apple juice. She liked this drink.

Julio showed Maxine around. They went to a higher level. Maxine noticed different rooms which had different compartments and living space for occupants on the space ship. Six beings from Clarion were walking around in the space ship. They had blonde or red hair. They were tall and slender. They also wore white or purple robes and sandals.

Maxine felt safe in the spaceship. The Clarions seemed friendly and harmless. They noticed Maxine.

They went on with their duties. Maxine walked near the Clarion occupants. She didn't speak to them. Yet, she sensed these celestial beings were communicating with her interiorly.

Once Maxine saw inside the spaceship she walked back to the entrance with Julio. She was impressed with her tour of this spaceship. She thanked Julio for showing her around. Julio walked back across the dunes with Maxine to the place where he first saw her in the dunes. Maxine thanked Julio again.

Julio spoke to Maxine before he departed to go back to his spaceship. He looked at her with compassion and said, "I will do my best to prevent the asteroids from crashing on the Earth." Maxine looked at Julio warmly. She said, "I am grateful you are capable of protecting the Earth."

Julio looked at Maxine once more. He said, "Goodbye. Have a good life. Maybe I will see you again someday." Julio walked away and went back to his spaceship. Once he reached his spaceship he stepped inside. The spaceship quickly lifted off the Earth and disappeared. Maxine thought about her unusual experience with a person from outer space.

Fiction

THIRTY

An Imaginary Experience

Sophie Washburn lived in Dublin, Ireland. She was 17 years old and she was attending high school in this city. Sophie had a vivid imagination. She often daydreamed while she attended school or sat under a tree in the park and nearby forests. Sophie wanted to travel but her parents did not have enough money to go on extensive trips around Europe and other parts of the world.

On Saturdays and Sundays after Sophie helped her mother around the house, she walked to a nearby park which had tall, shady, evergreen trees. She sat under her favorite tree to gaze at the trees and green grass in the park. As Sophia sat under a shady tree she began to dream.

Sophie took an imaginary trip in her dreams to an enchanted village near an enchanted forest. On her imaginary trip she saw elves and dwarves in an enchanted forest. They were dressed in elves and dwarves clothes.

Sophie observed the elves, who came out of the hollow trees. They danced around holding hands in a circle. They sang elves' songs. They appeared cheerful and happy. Sophie continued to observe them. The elves were able to see Sophie as she sat under a tree. They didn't appear to be afraid of her because she didn't try to attack them.

Then Sophie decided to talk to the elves. They stopped dancing and singing so they could listen to Sophie. Sophie said, "Hello. I like the way you sing and dance. Don't stop because of me." The elves decided to go on singing and dancing. Sophie sat there and enjoyed their dancing and singing.

Suddenly, some dwarves who were bigger than the elves, came into the enchanted forest. The dwarves were dressed in traditional folk costumes. The dwarves walked over to the elves and tried to scare them. The elves were frightened by the loud, threatening sounds the dwarves made. They rushed into the hollow trees to hide from the dwarves. They closed doors in the hollow trees to keep the dwarves out. Sophie witnessed the aggressive behavior of the dwarves. She was very concerned about the safety of the elves.

Sophie decided to scold the unfriendly dwarves. She said, "Leave the elves alone. They have a right to be here. You shouldn't try to scare them and frighten them away!" The dwarves laughed and made fun of Sophie. One dwarf said, "You don't belong here. Get out of our forest!" Sophie stood up. She was a good three feet taller than the dwarves. She walked toward the dwarves to frighten them away. The dwarves ran away from Sophie into the forest.

When all the dwarves had disappeared Sophie called to the elves. They were only half a foot tall. They came out of the hollow trees. The leader of the elves thanked Sophie for scaring the dwarves away. Then the elves began singing and dancing again. Sophie continued to observe the elves dance and sing.

THIRTY-ONE

Awareness About Nature

Being aware of Nature is a good way to become closer to God. Creations in nature are in existence everywhere. We need trees, grass, fruits and vegetables. Every creation in nature has a purpose for living on Earth.

An ecosystem exists in nature. Ecosystems keep a balance in nature. Creatures depend on each other to survive. Animals eat other animals as well as plants such as fruits and vegetation. Each living creature has the instinct to live. Each creature lives in a certain habitat and eats certain food. Some creatures live in hot or warm climates while other creatures live in cold or extremely cold climates. Creatures learn to survive in the climates they dwell in. They learn to gather food by hunting for it. They drink from streams and lakes.

Some creatures move from one place to another to find food. Birds build nests to dwell jn. Bears stay in caves and dig holes to dwell in. Coyotes and wolves dwell in hills. They stay close together to keep warm and raise their families. They howl at night to call to other wolves to let them know where they are. Cats stay in porches or in trees. House cats sleep indoors and go out of the house through cat holes in the walls or the door.

Many animals eat meat. Some are not meat eaters. They eat nuts, fruit, or vegetables. Fish eat other fishes as well as small crustaceans. They live in fresh water or ocean salt water. Fishes must live in water because they breathe through their gills.

Jungle animals must endure many dangers in the jungles. Lions, tigers, monkeys, gorillas, giraffes, zebras, gazelles anteaters, must learn to take care of themselves in a hot, humid, humid environment. Other animals such as sloths, leopards and panthers, dogs, cats, horses, mules, sheep, cows, calves, bulls , donkeys, bulls, and llamas graze in the fields and eat grass, foliage, hay, barley and wheat. Chickens, geese, ducks, turkeys and anteaters eat seeds, grass and scraps. Moorhens and other birds, and otters live in warmer climates. Otters eat fish and shell fish.

Desert creatures must endure an extremely hot, dry climate. They eat desert plants, insects, lizards, toad desert snakes, scorpions and insects that live in the desert. They hide under rocks in some shade. Some of them dwell near desert trees. They must search for water to stay alive.

There are many creatures and plants living on Earth. They continue to exist and expand as they grow and develop.

Fiction

THIRTY-TWO

Neighborly Deeds

To practice the Golden Rule by doing for others as you would like them to do unto you is a neighborly gesture. Good deeds help others who are in need of service and goodwill.

Wilma and Malcolm Brown lived in a neighborhood in Burbank, California. They were unfriendly and usually stayed away from their neighbors. They stayed in their house or backyard. When neighbors appeared nearby Wilma and Malcolm ignored them. They behaved this way for years.

Then, one day Wilma was home alone while Malcolm had gone downtown to do some business on his own. Wilma worked around the house. She decided to pick fruit off of some fruit trees in the backyard. She climbed in a taller fruit tree to reach for some apples. While she was reaching for apples she slipped off a branch and fell to the ground. She was unable to get up because she injured her legs. She couldn't stand and she was unable to walk. She was lying on the ground helpless.

Wilma became panicky because she was unable to get up. She screamed and yelled for help. Wilma yelled, "Help! Help! I need help! Wilma hoped someone would hear her. She waited for someone to come. No one came to help her. So, Wilma decided to call out again for help. She yelled as loud as she could. Wilma yelled, "Help! Help! Someone, please come quickly! I am hurt!" Wilma waited for someone nearby to come help her.

After a few more minutes a neighbor walked over to Wilma's yard. Wilma kept calling for help. The neighbor went to Wilma's backyard. He saw Wilma lying under an apple tree in her backyard. The neighbor walked over to Wilma. He asked, "Are you alright?" Wilma replied, "I am hurting badly." The neighbor asked, "What happened?" Wilma answered, "I fell out of this apple tree. I think my legs have been broken. I can't get up."

The neighbor realized that Wilma was in shock and that her legs had been injured. He carried a cell phone. He took out his cell phone and called paramedics to come and pick up Wilma. He told the paramedics Wilma's residential address. Then the neighbor waited with Wilma for the paramedics to arrive.

The neighbor introduced himself to Wilma. He said, "My name is Bill Porter. What is your name?" Wilma replied, "My name is Wilma Brown." Bill continued, "I live next door to you. I often thought of coming over to meet you. In fact, I attempted to meet you months ago. You didn't come to your door when I came over.

We finally are meeting each other." Wilma stared at Bill. She was in severe pain. She hoped her legs would mend. She was very uncomfortable. She wondered when the ambulance would arrive. Bill took off his jacket and covered Wilma up to keep her warmer.

The paramedics arrived fifteen minutes later. They brought a stretcher out of the ambulance. They walked into the backyard of Wilma's property. The paramedics brought the stretcher over to Wilma. They carefully placed Wilma in the stretcher. One of the paramedics covered Wilma with a warm blanket.

Bill Porter told the paramedics that Wilma had fallen out of the backyard apple tree. Wilma told the paramedics that her legs felt like they were broken. The paramedics expressed their concern. One of the paramedics said, "We are taking you to the hospital right now. You will receive care at the hospital." Wilma responded, "Will you tell my husband where I am?" Bill Porter spoke, "I will wait for your husband to come home. I will tell him where you are and why you went to the hospital." Bill asked, "What hospital will Wilma be taken to?" A paramedic answered, "We are taking the lady to the Burbank General Hospital." Bill said, "I will tell Wilma's husband that she is at the Burbank General Hospital."

The paramedics put Wilma in the ambulance. One paramedic sat near her. The other paramedic drove the ambulance to the hospital. Wilma thought about how Bill Porter came to her rescue. If he hadn't showed up she would have been lying in her backyard without help.

She realized that her neighbor had come over as soon as he heard her calling for help.

Bill waited for Malcolm Brown to come home. It was four hours before Malcolm drove into his driveway. Bill had been waiting next door at his house. As soon as Malcolm was in his driveway, Bill came over next door to his house. Bill told Malcolm that Wilma had fallen from a tree and that she was taken to the Burbank General Hospital.

Malcolm was very concerned. He thanked Bill Porter for letting him know what had happened to his wife. He got back into his car and drove to the Burbank General Hospital. He went into the hospital and investigated where his wife was in the hospital at the front desk. He wanted to see her right away to see how she was doing.

Malcolm was told what hospital room Wilma was in. He walked quickly down the hall to room 32. He entered this room. He saw Wilma lying in a hospital bed near the window. He walked over to his wife. She had her legs in casts. Wilma was glad to see her husband. Malcolm come over to her and said, "Wilma, I hope you are alright. What happened?" Wilma burst out into tears. Then she began to speak. She said, "I fell out of our apple tree in the backyard! I broke my legs when I fell. Our neighbor heard me calling in the backyard. He came over as soon as he heard me calling for help".

Malcolm was grateful that the neighbor came to help Wilma. He knew Wilma and he had not been friendly to the neighbors. Malcolm tried to console his wife while he was at the hospital

After five days, Wilma was released from the hospital. Malcolm took her back to their home. Her legs were still in casts. When she returned home, she called her neighbor, Bill Porter. She said, "Hello. Is this Bill Porter?" Bill answered, "Yes." Wilma said, "I want to thank you for coming over to look after me when I fell out of a tree in my backyard. I was cold and in severe pain. I realize how neighbors can be worth knowing. You are welcome to come to my house whenever you like." Bill responded, "I am glad I heard you in time!"

Wilma invited Bill Porter over to visit. Wilma served tea and cookies when Bill came over. Wilma was grateful that she had neighbors. Bill was glad Wilma was gradually recovering. She was able to use a walker. Then she used crutches to move around. Bill said he would keep an eye on her home to be sure she was safe. Wilma and Malcolm opened up from then on to their neighbors. They realized that neighbors are valuable and worth knowing. Neighborly deeds should be practiced in daily life.

Fiction

THIRTY-THREE

The Birthday Cards

Susan Fraser was going to be 21 years old. She had blond hair and brown eyes. She lived in La Jolla, California. She was just completing college near La Jolla. Her birthday was on March 7th. She hoped her family and friends would remember her twenty-first birthday.

Susan attended three classes on Monday, Wednesdays and Fridays. She attended two classes on Tuesdays and Thursdays. She was very busy at college attending classes. She worked part time to support her way through college. Her birthday was on a Saturday.

Susan began receiving birthday cards. Some birthday cards were store bought. Some birthday cards were hand made. Susan was impressed with most of the birthday cards.

There was an especially beautiful birthday card from Susan's male friend, Dale Lockner. Dale had designed a very beautiful birthday card with scenic flowers. Dale wrote a descriptive poem about Susan's birthday. When Susan opened this birthday card she was very impressed and overjoyed. This birthday card was one of the most unusual cards Susan had ever received.

When Dale came over to see Susan she thanked him for the lovely birthday card. She was happy that he had remembered her birthday. She didn't realize that Dale was so artistic. She planned to give him a beautiful, birthday card when his birthday came in September.

Dale took Susan out for her birthday. He took Susan to an expensive seafood restaurant in Santa Monica, California. Susan was excited about going to this elaborate, seafood restaurant. She got dressed up in a taffeta, purple dress with fancy gold shoes. She wore her hair up in a curly shape which made her face look more attractive.

Dale picked Susan up at 6 p.m. Saturday evening at her home. He drove a four door, silver Chrysler. Susan was ready when Dale arrived. She greeted him warmly. Dale and Susan went out to his car. He opened the front passenger door for Susan. She stepped into his car.

When Dale and Susan arrived in Santa Monica they got out of the car. Dale and Susan walked into the seafood restaurant. A host escorted them to a table near a window view. Once they were seated they studied the menus. A server came to their table to take their orders.

Susan decided to have a tuna steak, red potatoes, a medley of steamed vegetables and a raw, dark, green salad and herbal, iced tea. Dale ordered filet of sole, mashed potatoes, a medley of vegetables, a cup of clam chowder and hot coffee. The server brought the herb tea, coffee and whole wheat bread and butter first. Then she brought the soup and salad. Then the main course was brought to the table.

Susan and Dale were feasting and having a good time. Dale wished Susan Happy Birthday. He ordered some champagne to celebrate Susan's twenty-first birthday. When the champagne was brought to the table in a bucket of ice, Dale opened the bottle of champagne. He poured champagne into two champagne glasses.

Dale held up his champagne glass. So, Susan held up her champagne glass. Dale said, "Salute! Happy twenty-first birthday Susan!" Susan smiled. She said, "Thank you Dale." They both sipped the ice cold champagne. This was the first time Susan drank champagne in her life.

After the main course was completed, Susan and Dale were served birthday cake. There were candles on the cake. Susan made a wish and blew out the candles. The cake was cut and served to Susan and Dale. The cake was very delicious. Susan and Dale enjoyed the food and décor of this seafood restaurant. The view from the restaurant was quite scenic because Susan and Dale were able to see the scenic ocean and beach in the distance.

Dale and Susan had a wonderful time that night on their date. Susan felt this was the best birthday she had ever had. She was now twenty-one and she had her whole life ahead of her. She had fallen in love with Dale. She hoped he would ask her to marry him someday. She knew he was thoughtful as well as fun to be with.

Fiction

THIRTY-FOUR

Robin's Choices

Robin Wilkins grew up in a small town in New Jersey. She was the eldest of seven children. Robin grew up in a poor neighborhood. Her parents were financially poor. Robin had to go without luxuries.

Other families had things Robin's family didn't have. The Wilkins family managed to have just enough food, a roof over their heads and clothing. Robin was used to having very little. Yet, she accepted her impoverished situation.

Robin tried to make good choices. For instance, she chose to work part time while she was in high school. She tried to make the best choices about how to study efficiently. She had little or no time to socialize because she was so busy working at a part time job plus going to school. She needed time to do her homework.

Robin made the choice to go to college after high school. She chose to study hard so she was prepared for high school exams. She completed high school with above average grades. Robin planned to go to junior college first to complete her general education courses first.

After Robin graduated from high school she registered at a nearby junior college for the Fall quarter. She had been saving money to pay for her college tuition. Robin signed up for three courses of general education. She continued to work part time while she attended junior college. Robin had little time to socialize with others because she was so busy going to college and working.

Robin completed the two year general education program. She earned above average grades. Robin transferred to a university in the city where she lived. She continued to complete upper division courses. She made the choice to become a zoology director. She majored in zoology "which is the science, a branch of biology that deals with animals and characteristics or properties of animals or animal groups" as defined in Webster's New Word Dictionary.

Robin managed to continue working while she completed her upper division courses. She never let up in pursuing her goal to finish college. Within three years Robin completed her zoology courses and related subjects. She received a B.S. degree in Zoology.

While searching for a job in Zoology Robin chose to try to become employed at a large zoo in San Diego, California. She began by caring for the animals at the zoo. Over a period of seven years Robin looked after many zoo animals. She fed and bathed them. She cleaned animal cages by taking a hose to wash each cage floor and walls. She moved the animals into different cages.

Robin became familiar with all the animals at the San Diego Zoo. In fact, Robin was liked by the Zoo animals because she met their needs and gave them enough attention. Robin became popular at the San Diego Zoo.

Robin became familiar with all the animals at the San Diego Zoo. In fact, Robin was liked by the Zoo animals because she met their needs and gave them enough attention. Robin became popular at the San Diego Zoo.

When Robin had worked at the San Diego Zoo for ten years the director of this zoo retired. Robin decided to apply for the director position at the San Diego Zoo. She waited to hear from the employment committee about their decision regarding this job.

Several days later Robin received a letter which stated she had been selected to become the next zoo director at the San Diego Zoo. Robin was overjoyed and happy to be selected to be the next zoo director. Each choice Robin made, step by step, led to her opportunity to become a zoo director someday.

Fiction

THIRTY-FIVE

Unusual Dreams

We have had unusual dreams from time to time. We may dream about something we have experienced or are emotionally attached to and concerned about. Unusual dreams may be about extraordinary issues and experiences.

We can learn about people, places and situations even in our dreams. Unusual dreams take us to spectacular places in other dimensions. For instance, Julia Stevens dreamed that she left her physical body and began flying high in the sky around the Earth above clouds in her astral body. She could see the landscape many miles above in the sky as she looked down. This vivid view of the clouds that were rolling along with puffy pink and orange colors was interesting to observe as Julia flew above them. Julia could see many views of landscapes such as forests, lakes, meadows, mountains and oceans. Julia was amazed at the many views of the

Earth's surface. She felt a sense of freedom. Flying in the upper atmosphere was a magnificent experience for Julia. She became aware of nature's plan around the Earth's surface.

Julia continued to experience unusual dreams. Her parents had passed away several years ago. Julia had a dream about her parents. She saw them in her dreams frequently. They appeared before her and spoke to her in various dreams. Julia felt that her parents were still alive because of her dreams about them. Julia felt close to her parents. It was as if they were still alive.

Julia's mother spoke to Julia in several dreams. She said, "I am glad to be where I am. I felt like I am still on the Earth. Yet, it is much nicer here. No one fights or treats others badly. I don't have to worry about cooking, cleaning house or paying taxes! I can move around freely and do what I want to do. I am not suffering from illnesses. I don't feel any pain." Julia listened intently to her mother. She was glad her mother was happy in another dimension. She was no longer afraid to pass away.

Julia asked her mother, "Does the dimension you have gone to look just like the Earth?" Julia's mother replied, "Where I am looks very much like the Earth. Yet, it is prettier here. You will like this dimension when you pass over here."

Julia also dreamed about her father. When her father appeared before her in dreams, Julia felt he was still living on Earth. He looked younger and he seemed freer and happier. Julia's father said, "Hello Julia. Are you well?" Julia answered, "Yes, I am well Dad. How are you?" Julia's father answered, "I am well and happy here. Your mother and I see one another. So, I am happy to be here. Everyone here is friendly. I feel at peace here. You will like it here when you leave the physical world. Be happy on Earth while you are there."

Julia thought about what her parents told her. She looked forward to being with her parents someday. Meanwhile, she had a purpose for living on the physical plane. She had karma known as cause and effect to fulfill. She was only thirty-five. She had her physical life ahead of her to experience. Julia was pleased that she had vivid dreams about her parents. She was able to see unusual astral places which were quite beautiful such as lovely flower gardens, pillars of light and a rose ocean rolling back and forth. The sun was bright yellow and white. Yet, the sun did not hurt her eyes. Purple mist moved around over the astral sky. Trees were more symmetrical and geometrical with blue and purple leaves and golden trunks. Flowers were celestial looking. Celestial music could be heard. It was very peaceful in this dimension.

Fiction

THIRTY-SIX

Adventures At Sea

Norman Skyman liked to sail in the sea. He was an adventurer and navigator who enjoyed traveling long distances across different oceans. He had purchased a large motorboat which he supplied with sailing supplies, equipment and appropriate clothing. Because he was so adventurous he frequently navigated to far away places across the sea.

Norman lived in San Diego, California, which is known for large, marine boats. Tourists are able to walk into different, historical vessels. Norman had been on all of these vessels in the harbor of San Diego as a boy. His experiences on these vessels motivated him to become a sailor and navigator on the high seas. Norman observed many instruments and different sections of these large vessels.

After Norman supplied his large, cabin cruiser motorboat which had a main cabin, kitchenette, bed loft and storage room plus a refrigerator, stove and cupboards, he was ready to navigate. He also had sails available in case his motor malfunctioned on his boat. Norman had a compass so he knew what direction to sail in. He turned on the motor to his boat to warm it up.

Once the motor of Norman's boat was warmed up he headed out of the harbor of San Diego in a westward direction. It was a sunny day with a few clouds in the sky. Norman continued navigating his motor boat across the ocean towards the Hawaiian Islands. He navigated for many miles in the ocean. His boat moved over rippling currents of cold water. He noticed white caps on the ocean.

As Norman navigated on the ocean, clouds began to roll in above in the sky. He continued his journey. Some pelicans and seagulls flew over his boat. Several seagulls landed on his boat deck to rest. Norman didn't try to scare them away. He knew the seagulls needed a place to land to dwell for awhile. Then Norman saw some whales spouting as they came to the surface of the ocean. They dipped their large tails up and down into the ocean. Some dolphins finally appeared. They swam close to Norman's boat.

When many dark clouds had appeared in the sky, it began to rain heavily. Waves were lapping against Norman's motorboat as he moved along across the turbulent sea. He navigated all day towards the Hawaiian Islands. It continued to rain for many hours. Norman had put on a raincoat and rain hat to keep the sopping rain from drenching his clothes.

Finally, the rain stopped. The ocean was still choppy. Norman's motorboat moved up and down over the rough currents. He stopped his motorboat for awhile in order to make a late lunch. He prepared baked salmon, baked red potatoes, a dark green lettuce salad with sliced tomatoes, carrots, celery and green peppers. He buttered some sourdough bread. He also prepared some hot coffee. Norman sat at a table in the cabin of the boat to eat his meal. He was very hungry because he hadn't eaten for many hours. He had only eaten toast, several eggs and sliced apple pieces for breakfast.

After Norman was finished with his late afternoon meal, he cleaned up the kitchenette and table in the cabin. He listened to a radio on his boat. He turned on the daily forecast and news. The newscaster said there would be more rain storms in the Pacific Ocean. A big storm was headed in Norman's direction. He would have to keep overlapping waves from flooding his boat.

Norman turned on the motor to his boat. Seagulls had continued landing on his boat. The motorboat moved across the ocean again as Norman controlled the steering wheel. The seagulls heard the loud sound of the motor. Many of them flew away when they heard this loud sound. Norman continued his journey to Hawaii. He would have to navigate many more hours because he had traveled only half way there.

Darker clouds appeared in the sky. Another ocean squall formed. Norman navigated across the ocean squall. His motorboat was hit by strong currents of rolling ocean waves. Norman became worried that his boat might be damaged by the ocean storm. It lasted for many hours. Norman held onto the steering wheel carefully. He had to control the boat especially because of the swift storm.

After many hours of ocean currents hitting his boat, Norman began to see a clearing ahead. He was concerned about the boat capsizing because of the turbulent gale in the ocean. Fortunately he was able to navigate his boat out of the horrendous storm. Once he was in calmer waters he felt safe. He hoped he had enough fuel to make it to Hawaii. He continued on for hours until he came to what he thought were the Hawaiian Islands. However, because of the storm his boat was swept off course. He ended up at an island northwest of the Hawaiian Islands called Palmyra Island. This was not a tourist island.

Palmyra Island had Norfolk Pine trees and some tropical palm trees. It was somewhat cooler than the Hawaiian Islands. Norman anchored his motorboat close to the shore. He lowered a canoe with some picnic food stored in the canoe. He got into the canoe and paddled to shore. Once he was at the edge of the beach he pulled his canoe onto dry beach sand away from the water.

Norman laid a big towel on the beach. He brought prepared tuna sandwiches with lettuce, pickles and mayonnaise from a picnic basket. He opened sealed potato chips and a ice cold cola soda. Norman sat on the towel and ate his tuna sandwich. He opened a bag of potato chips to eat. He sipped the ice cold cola. Norman glanced around the beach and shore. The beach was deserted. After he ate his sandwich, potato chips and drank his cola, Norman picked up the towel and picnic basket to put in his canoe. He decided to explore the beach and went further into the interior of Palmyra Island.

It was quiet on this island. Norman was curious if people lived here because he was alone. He hoped to see some people as he looked around. As he walked deep into the Norfolk Pine forest he heard tropical birds chirping. He saw colorful birds flying around in the forest. They were multi-colored with interesting beaks. Some tropical birds flew quickly away from Norman. They seemed to be frightened when they saw him walking through the pine forest. Norman continued walking until he came to the other side of the forest.

There was a clearing on the other side of the island. Norman saw thatched roof huts. There were island people moving near the huts. The huts were made of palm leaves, bamboo and other plant fibers. The islanders noticed Norman coming towards their village. These villagers stopped what they were doing and stared at Norman. They wondered who he was and wondered why he was approaching them. Norman sensed that these islanders were not used to seeing strangers.

Norman walked closer and closer to the islanders. Finally he stood before them. Several native women were standing near him. He looked very different than the island men on Palmyra Island. Norman didn't have any jewelry, shells or ornaments to offer them. He decided to say hello to these island people who had brown skin, long black kinky hair and dark brown eyes. Norman was very surprised that these islanders understood English. Some of them answered by saying, "Hello."

A female villager said, "Who are you?" Norman replied, "My name is Norman." She asked, "Why are you here?" Norman responded, "I came here on my boat. I thought I was coming to the Hawaiian Islands. Where am I?" The woman villager answered, "You are on Palmyra Island. I don't know where the Hawaiian Islands are. I have never been off Palmyra Island."

Norman realized that these islanders lived simple lives. Norman didn't see any cars or airplanes. There were island made boats on the beach ready to be used for fishing. They didn't even know where the Hawaiian Islands were. He would have to search for the Hawaiian Islands on his own. Norman asked, "Have you lived on this island all your lives?" A male islander stepped forward and spoke. "Our people have lived on this island for many years. Our ancient ancestors came here on boats. We have been here ever since. Do you plan to stay here?" Norman replied, "I live in San Diego, California. I plan to navigate on my boat back to California when I leave Palmyra Island."

One of the island women invited Norman to sit down near her hut. Norman accepted her invitation and followed her to her hut. The island women said, "My name is Kikia. What is your name?" Norman replied, "My name is Norman." Kikia offered Norman some mango fruit. He was still somewhat hungry even though he had eaten an hour ago. Norman accepted the mango fruit. He began eating this juicy, delicious fruit. He felt refreshed after eating this tropical fruit.

Kikia continued to be friendly to Norman. She was attracted to Norman. Kikia prepared some steamed, island fish with island rice. Norman ate the fish and rice plus some island eggplant. It was delicious. Norman appreciated the way Kikia cooked. He was attracted to her. He had not expected to meet a Palmyra islander who was so attractive.

After Norman was finished eating he decided to stay near Kikia. He wanted to know her better. Kikia appeared to be around twenty years old. She had long black hair, brown eyes and light brown skin. She had a beautiful figure. She appeared very healthy and youthful.

Norman stayed in the island village the rest of the day. In the evening the villagers built a big fire outside near the village. The islanders gathered near the fire. They began to chant in their island language. Then they joined hands and began to dance their traditional dances. Norman enjoyed watching these islanders dance in their native dances. Kikia joined the other islanders and danced with them. The dancing continued for several hours. Norman was encouraged by Kikia to join in with everyone as they danced. He decided to dance with the islanders. He observed them dance and he learned to follow their body movements and footsteps. He really enjoyed their traditional dances.

When the Moon had come out and the fire had simmered down the islanders stopped to rest. Norman was welcome to stay in their village. He slept outside near the fire to keep warm that night. He thought about Kikia. He was growing fond of her. He finally fell asleep. The next morning Kikia prepared Norman's breakfast. She invited Norman to eat with her at her hut. They ate fresh papaya, kiwi fruit and drank guava juice.

Norman became more familiar with Kikia. Kikia told Norman what she learned about her island lifestyle and how she grew up with certain customs and beliefs. Norman told Kikia how he grew up with American customs and beliefs. Norman and Kikia communicated effectively.

Kikia showed Norman around Palmyra Island. They went fishing and swimming together. They gathered fruit and island vegetables. Kikia continued to prepare meals for Norman. He stayed at Kikia's village for three weeks. Norman began to know the villagers more and more every day. He especially became acquainted with Kikia.

Norman had fallen in love with Kikia. He listened to her sing island songs. He had danced with her at night almost every night that he was on Palmyra Island. After three weeks, Norman felt it was time to leave Palmyra Island. Norman wanted to return to San Diego, California. Norman wanted to take Kikia back with him to San Diego. He told her that he wanted her to come with him to California. Kikia wanted to come with Norman. She loved him. She had never been away from Palmyra or her people before. She had to make a decision whether she would go with Norman or remain on Palmyra Island.

Norman persuaded Kikia to go with him to California. Kikia collected her clothes and a few other belongings. She looked around Palmyra Island for the last time. Then Kikia stepped on Norman's boat. He warmed up the motor. He checked his compass. Then he headed out to sea in a northeastern direction towards California.

It would take three days and two nights for Norman and Kikia to return across the Pacific Ocean to California. Norman and Kikia enjoyed beautiful sunrises and spectacular sunsets. The ocean remained much calmer during the journey across the Pacific Ocean. There were rolling waves and one small storm. Kikia prepared food on the boat. Norman showed Kikia how to use the stove and how to store food in the refrigerator and freezer. Kikia learned to prepare different American meals on her journey across the ocean.

When Norman and Kikia arrived in San Diego Norman made plans to marry Kikia. They were married within three days. Kikia stayed at Norman's house in San Diego overlooking San Diego Harbor. They were happy together. Kikia missed her family and island villagers. Yet, she was able to make a new life for herself in San Diego. She learned to adapt to her new surroundings. Norman and Kikia had a successful marriage.

THIRTY-SEVEN

Bedtime Stories

Alice and Brian Snokley had three children, Aaron, Betsy and Owen. Their children were age 2, 3 and 5. Often, before bedtime, Alice or Brian took turns telling bedtime stories to their three children. As a result, their children settled down better and were willing to fall asleep after they heard some fascinating stories.

It was Brian's turn to tell bedtime stories. Aaron, Betsy and Owen slept in the same bedroom. Their beds were arranged close together. Brian sat near all three children. He began telling bedtime stories. He told a story about <u>Goldilocks and the Three Bears.</u> He said Goldilocks wandered through some woods. She came to a cabin. She knocked on the door. No one answered. So, Goldilocks walked into the cabin. She saw three chairs at a dining room table. She sat at Papa Bear's chair. It was too big. Then she sat at Mama Bear's chair. It was still too big. Then she sat at Baby Bear's chair. It was just right. She had tasted Papa Bear's porridge which was too hot. Then she had tasted Mama Bear's porridge which was too cold. When she tasted Baby Bear's porridge it was just right. So, she ate up Baby Bear's porridge.

Goldilocks was tired. So she walked into a bedroom. She saw three beds. She lay down on Papa Bear's bed. It was too hard. Then Goldilocks lay down on Mama Bear's bed. It was too soft. Then Goldilocks lay down on Baby Bear's bed. It was just right. Goldilocks fell sound asleep. While Goldilocks was sleeping Papa, Mama and Baby Bear came home. They noticed their porridge had been tasted and Baby Bear's porridge was gone. They walked into the bedroom. Papa Bear said, "Who has been sleeping in my bed?" Mama Bear asked, "Who has been sleeping in my bed?" Baby Bear looked at his bed. He saw Goldilocks sleeping in his bed. Baby Bear said, "Someone is sleeping in my bed!" Goldilocks woke up. She saw Papa Bear, Mama Bear and Baby Bear. She was frightened. So, she got out of Baby Bear's bed quickly and ran out of the bedroom. She ran outside and ran through the forest away from the three bears' home. Papa Bear, Mama Bear and Baby Bear never saw Goldilocks again.

When Brian had finished telling his story to his three children they didn't want to go to sleep. Alice and Brian told their children they must go to sleep. Brian and Alice tucked their children in their beds. They hugged and kissed each of them. Brian turned off the light in their room. Alice closed their door as Brian and Alice left their room. They said goodnight before they left their bedroom. Alice and Brian went into the living room. Brian spoke to his wife, Alice. "It's your turn to tell a bedtime story tomorrow night!" Alice looked at Brian and smiled. She said, "I know. I will have to tell a different bedtime story tomorrow night." Alice and Brian relaxed on the living room couch.

THIRTY-EIGHT

Bear Country

Bears have roamed around the countryside of America, Canada and Alaska. Alaska has become a state of America. There are black, brown and white bears that have lived and dwelled in Bear Country. Bears claim certain territories in order to hunt for food. They hunt for fish such as salmon at running streams. They gather wild berries, roots and scraps of human, prepared food. Bears drink water from streams, lakes and creeks as well as ponds and puddles.

Bears like to eat honey. They hunt for honey in trees. Bees produce honey from pollen and nectar. Honey can be found in beehives. Bears usually find caves to sleep in especially during wintertime. Some bears walk up to mountainsides to locate caves. They may sleep outside near rocks and under trees. When it rains or snows they stay in caves or dig deep holes to dwell in.

During hibernation bears find a protective shelter to stay in during cold winter months. They usually give birth to two or three bear cubs. The bear cubs nurse during winter months from the mother cub in order to grow and develop physically. The bear cubs are blind at birth. They cling to their mothers for protection. They are helpless at birth. So, bear cubs depend on their mother bears to feed them and keep them warm in caves during many cold winter months in freezing weather.

When Spring comes the mother bear takes her cubs outside into the meadows to eat grass, berries and to hunt for rodents. Bear cubs observe their mother bears hunt. They learn how to hunt step by step until they can hunt by themselves.

Many bears live in Denali National Park in Alaska. Many bears live in the wilderness in forests, near oaks and streams as well as mountaintops in caves and on slopes. Bears grow a lot of fur which keeps them warmer. Bears are able to endure severe weather. They are feared by smaller creatures and people because they are much larger and stronger. Bears have strong, sharp teeth. They have sharp claws which they use to attack their victims. Bears can be very dangerous.

Some bears wander into campgrounds looking for food. They tend to steal any food they can find in the campsites. They look in garbage cans for garbage to eat. Some bears may knock tents down while they search for food. Bears have been known to attack people who travel in the wilderness.

Bears have lived in the United States of America for thousands of years before human beings arrived here. Bears roamed freely without being hunted down by human hunters. There were thousands of bears moving around in the wilderness which was bear country.

THIRTY-NINE

Music Can Uplift You

Music was created to stimulate listeners to listen to melodies and background accompliments. Religious songs have a healing effect. Religious words can uplift the mind and emotions. Such songs are THE HOLY CITY, THE MESSIAH, THE LORD'S PRAYER, THE TWENTY-THIRD PSALM and more. These famous, spiritual songs have been sung many times during religious holidays as well as in many churches on Sundays.

Music should uplift us. If music is harmonious and pleasant we can relax and become inspired by the quality of the music. If music is harsh and not melodic it may not uplift and inspire us. So, we shouldn't listen to inharmonious music.

The original, musical compositions of Chopin, Mozart, Beethoven, Debussy, Handel, Mendelssohn, Haydn, Bach, Dvorak, Ravel, and other classical composers can uplift us. They have composed very melodic, harmonious music.

Many Broadway hits are uplifting such as <u>Brigadoon</u>, <u>On A Clear Day You Can See Forever</u>, <u>Try to Remember</u>, <u>September Song</u>, <u>Camelot</u>, <u>If Ever I Should Leave You</u>, <u>Kismet</u>, <u>The Sound of Music</u>, <u>I Could Have Danced All Night</u>, <u>Summertime</u>, <u>Oklahoma</u>, <u>Tomorrow</u>, <u>Autumn Leaves</u>, <u>Chances Are</u> and more. We feel and hear these melodic songs which can lift us up emotionally.

Each composer has his or her own musical style. Yet, if the music is pleasant, harmonious and melodic we enjoy listening to it.

Nonfiction

FORTY

Contemporary Superstars

ELIZABETH TAYLOR

Elizabeth Taylor was born in February 27, 1932 in London, England. Elizabeth Taylor began as a child actress. She signed up with MGM and remained with this studio for almost twenty years. She appeared in films such as LASSIE COME HOME and NATIONAL VELVET as a child, which were popular box office hits.

Elizabeth Taylor continued to act as an adult in FATHER OF THE BRIDE and A PLACE IN THE SUN. She won an Oscar for BUTTERFIELD 8. She co-starred with Paul Newman in CAT ON A HOT TIN ROOF. She also acted in GIANT and WHO'S AFRAID OF VIRGINIA WOOLF.

In the 1980s, Elizabeth Taylor acted in a stage play written by Lillian Hellman entitled THE LITTLE FOXES. Elizabeth was a strikingly beautiful woman with purple-blue eyes and black ebony hair. She became even more well known in LITTLE WOMEN, SUDDENLY, LAST SUMMER, CLEOPATRA and TAMING OF A SHREW.

Elizabeth Taylor was married eight times. She was married to James Hilton, Michael Wilding, Mike Todd, Eddie Fisher, Richard Burton (twice), John Ford and someone twenty years younger than herself. Mike Todd was killed. Elizabeth married Richard Burton two times. They were divorced twice.

Elizabeth Taylor experienced illnesses and tragedies. She fell off a horse when she was in NATIONAL VELVET at age 12. When Todd was killed in a plane crash Elizabeth suffered from this tragedy. She suffered from tumors in her brain in her early seventies. She also has had several hip surgeries which has handicapped her.

Elizabeth Taylor lives in Bel Air, California near Beverly Hills up in the hills in a lovely home away from the road. Her gate is closed and locked to the general public. She has a view of woods. She has a swimming pool, which she exercises in.

DEBORAH KERR

Deborah Kerr was born in 1921 in Helensburgh, Dumbarton, Scotland. Deborah Kerr has red hair and was the daughter of a Scottish architect. Deborah attended drama school in Bristol, England where one of her performances won her a ballet scholarship at

Sadler's Wells. She was interested in studying ballet but she was too old to train seriously for ballet. However, she obtained walk-in parts at the open-air theatre in Regent's Park.

Deborah Kerr performed in CONTRABAND in 1940. Then she was in Gabriel Pascal's MAJOR BARBARA. After this Deborah starred in LOVE ON THE DOLE which was about a down-trodden working-class girl. Powell and Press Burger gave her a triple role in THE LIFE AND DEATH OF COLONEL BLIMP. Deborah Kerr played a nun in BLACK NARCISSUS.

In 1947, Deborah Kerr went to Hollywood and played in major roles such as FROM HERE TO ETERNITY and THE KING AND I. She also starred in THE SUNDOWNERS, PERFECT STRANGERS, VACATION FROM MARRIAGE, TEA AND SYMPATHY, HEAVEN KNOWS MR. ALLISON, SEPARATE TABLES and THE ARRANGEMENT.

Deborah Kerr's abundant acting talent was evident in both drama and comedy. She is a very successful actress. She has sung and danced in different films. She has been a superstar for many years. She was eighty-nine in 2010.

GREGORY PECK

Gregory Peck was born in 1916 in La Jolla, California. Gregory Peck graduated from the Neighborhood Playhouse in New York. Peck was on Broadway in 1942 in Emlyn Williams' THE MORNING STAR. Then two years later he played a Russian partisan in Jacques Toourneur's DAYS OF GLORY. THE KEYS OF THE KINGDOM brought Gregory stardom which continued for nearly 40 years.

Gregory Peck played heroic figures of integrity and who reflected Gregory's own liberal opinions. Gregory Peck was tall, handsome, rugged, yet gentle. He played a Southern lawyer standing up to racialism in TO KILL A MOCKINGBIRD in which he received an Oscar award. He was a major actor in SPELL BOUND, THE PARADIVE CASE, TWELVE O'CLOCK HIGH, THE GUNFIGHTER, THE BOYS FROM BRAZIL, GENTLEMAN'S AGREEMENT, ROMAN HOLIDAY, THE MAN IN THE GRAY FLANNEL SUIT, THE BIG COUNTRY, THE STALLING MOON, THE DOVE, PORK CHOP HILL, BELOVED INFIDEL, THE SNOWS OF KILLIMANJARO, THE SEA WOLF, THE GUNS OF NAVARONE, MAROONED and more. F r o m 1967 to 1970 Gregory Peck was President of the Academy of Motion Picture Arts and Sciences. Gregory Peck became a superstar. He has been recognized for many of his acting roles in a variety of films.

FORTY-ONE

Some Musical Instruments

Playing a harmonica takes musical skills and techniques. Harmonicas are different sizes. Some harmonicas weigh more than other harmonicas.

A harmonica is a musical instrument consisting of a conveniently arranged series of graduated glasses from which tones are produced by rubbing the edges with a wet finger. It is a former percussion instrument consisting of metal or glass stripes which were struck with small mallets. A harmonica is a small wind instrument played with the mouth. It is a mouth organ which has a series of graduated metal reeds that vibrate and produce tones when air is blown or sucked across them.

Accordions are musical instruments with keys, metal reeds and bellows. It is played by alternately pulling out and pressing together the bellows to force air through the reeds, which are opened by fingering the keys. Lawrence Welk learned to play an accordion when he was a boy.

His father taught him to play the accordion. Lawrence Welk became a well known accordion player. Evidently, Lawrence formed his own band.

The Lawrence Welk Show existed in the 1950s. Lawrence Welk was the band leader. His band played popular music. Lawrence played his accordion with the band. He wrote a book entitled WONDERFUL WONDERFUL about his life and his music career.

A clavichord is a stringed musical instrument with a keyboard, predecessor of the piano. A clavichord has horizontal strings generally of equal length which are struck at various points from below by metal wedges at the end of each key, producing soft tones with limited dynamics. It has been called a harpsichord. Clavichords were played before pianos were produced.

FORTY-TWO

Miraculous Wonders

Miraculous wonders exist on the Earth and other dimensions. Rainbows, which reflect a variety of bright colors, are wonders. Dewdrops sparkle on grass and leaves with diamond-like effects. Colorful gems hidden in the ground are magnificent to look at when they are discovered and polished. Pearls, jade, amethyst stones, gypsum, opals, diamonds, gold, silver and ruby red stones are spectacular to gaze at.

The ebb and flow of ocean waves fascinate viewers. The Moon glows with reflecting circles of light around it. Bright moonlight stands out in the night sky. The sun shines so brightly we are unable to look at its dazzling light directly with our eyes. Yet, the wonder of the sun's light produces necessary energy so we can live on Earth.

Miraculous wonders exist in the nature kingdom. Golden crested peacocks as well as colorful plumed peacocks, pink flamingos, cockatoos, parakeets, parrots and other colorful, tropical birds are especially beautiful. Striped tigers and spotted leopards appear vivid with their dynamic colors.

Elephants descend from an ancient ancestry for millions of years. Elephants are very intelligent with wonderful memories. They have roamed on different continents. Their enormous bodies are marvelous. Elephants are able to work by carrying logs across waterways, etc. Elephants carry passengers long distances. They are dressed up in special costumes to walk in parades during religious ceremonies and for holiday celebrations.

Sunrises and sunsets are marvelous wonders. Their brilliant, vivid colors of orange, pink, yellow, purple and red are magnificent to observe. Clouds spread out with puffy designs of orange, pink, yellow and white arrays of colors. Their artistic designs are wondrous to behold.

Waterfalls are fabulous to observe with water flowing, sparkling, fresh water falling down mountainsides and steep hills. Waterfalls flow into streams, oceans and large creeks. Sunrise and sunset colors reflect in waterfalls adding miraculous color schemes to the flowing water.

Other miraculous wonders are different forests and national parks around the world. Evergreen trees such as pine, spruces, elms, redwoods, silver pines, Norfolk pines and cedars grow in clusters, groves and forests. Eucalyptus trees and palm trees add much beauty to the Earth's landscapes. Trees hold the soil down and stops erosion. Trees are miraculous wonders on Earth. Fan trees are unusual, palm trees.

Fiction

FORTY-THREE

Fond Memories

Fond memories help us to adjust to life as well as to help us maintain balance and equilibrium. We can recall fond, special moments in our lives. We are able to remember birthday celebrations, Christmas holidays, festivals, traveling adventures and personal moments with loved ones.

Nathan Weatherly was 76 years old. He had a dynamic, memorable life. He had acquired many interests and hobbies. He was interested in traveling around the world. He had collected rare specimens such as unusual rocks, meteorites, gemstones and different types of leaves. He even collected unusual relics and antiques.

Nathan enjoyed studying and touching his collection of rocks, meteorites, gemstones, and leaves. Nathan had a collection of gold and silver coins which he displayed in glass cases. He admired his coin collections. He had coins which were hundreds of years old. Some of Nathan's coins were very valuable. Nathan didn't advertise that he had valuable coins. He didn't want to be robbed.

Nathan enjoyed playing golf, tennis, volleyball and baseball. He recalled how he won many tennis matches, golf tournaments and pitched for baseball games. He remembered participating in volleyball teams. Sports were an important part of Nathan's life. He had flashbacks of different sports he participated in.

Other fond memories Nathan had were his experiences in tasting gourmet foods in exotic restaurants. He enjoyed marinated, buttered lobster, shrimp and calamari steaks. He enjoyed baked Alaska, peach cobbler, lasagna with a variety of meats and cheeses. Nathan enjoyed organic salads with spinach, dark green lettuce, watercress, celery, radishes, carrots, baby tomatoes, green and red sliced peppers with a homemade dressing with herbs, olive oil and mild spices.

Traveling was one of Nathan's favorite pastimes. He recalled many fond memories of unusual places he had traveled to. He especially recalled traveling inside China, India and the South Sea Islands. He recalled walking inside the Great Wall. He was able to see for miles as he walked up stone steps. The Great Wall of China was many miles long. The Great Wall was constructed to keep enemies and intruders out of China. Nathan recalled going to the Forbidden City. He recalled walking up steep steps into the Emperor's palace. He saw the Emperor's golden throne with dragons designed on it. He saw the palace chambers which were elegant. There were high ceilings with indoor columns. The Forbidden

City was surrounded with Chinese gardens and different Chinese pagodas and servant chambers. Nathan still thought about the Forbidden City with awe.

In India, Nathan recalled his visits to different Indian temples. Meditation rooms existed inside of each temple. Burnt incense permeated each temple. Visitors and Indians sat on the floor facing an altar with statues of Hindu gods. Fruit and miniature bells were on the altars. Burning incense could be seen on the altars. Nathan meditated in some of the Hindu and Brahman temples in different cities and sanctuaries in India. He traveled to Bombay, New Delhi and Agra. He had become aware of Indian customs and beliefs. He recalled how happy and peaceful the people of India appeared to be because they prayed to their gods regularly.

In the South Seas, Nathan remembered viewing vivid sunrises and sunsets. He recalled how friendly the Polynesian people were. Their Polynesian dances were unique. They dressed in grass skirts and wore flowers and colorful head dresses. Polynesian women and men moved their feet and hands rhythmically while drums were played. Nathan especially enjoyed observing Polynesian dancers.

Nathan had lived a happy and adventurous life. He had many fond memories of his adventures around the world as well as the United States of America.

FORTY-FOUR

Melodrama Experience

Melodramas were very popular in the 18th and 19th centuries. There are heroes and villains in the melodramas. The audience is encouraged to say boo or hurrah when characters are acting on the stage.

In Oceano, California, there is a Melodrama theatre. People buy theatre tickets in advance or at the theatre door. Usually 50 to 80 people or more attend melodrama productions. A variety of dramatic topics such as CHRISTMAS EXTRAVAGANZA, ROMEO AND JULIET, MR. SCROOGE, HAMLET, LUMBERJACK IN LOVE THANKSGIVING IS HERE and SLEEPY HOLLOW AWAKENS, etc.

In the 18th and 19th centuries there was no television or radios. DVDs and VCRS did not exist during those centuries. So, melodramas, operas and regular dramas were the main form of entertainment. Many people attended melodramas, operas and regular stage plays.

In SLEEPY HOLLOW AWAKENS the main character comes down with sleeping sickness. He falls asleep. Meanwhile, other characters around him are concerned that he fell asleep and wouldn't wake up. Time goes by and many changes take place. For instance, his brothers and sisters grew up. He also grew older. In time, when he was an adult he grew a beard even while he was sleeping. His beard grew very long. Finally, his beard turned gray and then white.

Finally, the main character woke up after many years. He noticed how his brothers and sisters were much older. His parents had passed away. The main character realized he was no longer a child. He was in his late sixties with a white beard. All that time had gone by while he was sleeping. He finally had awakened from a deep slumber.

FORTY-FIVE

Light Within

Light within heals us. Light within enlightens us. Light within awakens us. We need light to stay alive. We thrive from light. We depend on light in order to survive.

Many people need pure white light to bring peace and harmony into their lives. White light is filled with wisdom, God's awareness and love. White light is the salvation for the world. White light exists in every living thing. Without light life could not exist. We depend on light every second.

Look within to become aware of light. Know God within. God is a supreme being of light. To know god is very important. Our lives should be centered on our God presence. We should become aware of our Father-Mother God. We should learn to know our Christ Self. The Christ Self listens to the I Am Presence. We should learn to listen to the still small voice of God with one's consciousness. We should learn to listen regularly to our still small voice.

White light is eternal. It permeates throughout the Cosmos. White light may exist on other planets and in other galaxies and in every solar system. So, focus on white light within. Realize God within. Become one with all life.

Nonfiction

FORTY-SIX

Zebras Are Interesting

Zebras have white and black stripes. They live in the savannahs of Africa. Zebras are mammals. They are related to horses. They have four legs with hooves on their lower legs.

Zebras stay together usually as they graze in fields. They eat wild grass, leaves and other vegetation. They usually sleep at night when it is dark. During sunrise until sunset they graze and look after their young zebras.

Zebras have to be on guard when there are lions, tigers and panthers nearby. Lions, tigers and panthers kill young zebras to eat. They chase after them and knock them down. When they are helpless they kill them.

Zebras have existed in Africa for thousands of years. They have survived and reproduced. Many zebras have been put in zoos and in Safari parks. They are able to live in very warm climates as well as mild climates. They do not live in severely cold climates.

Zebras eat barley, hay and oats in zoos as well as grass. They drink fresh water usually. Zebras live at least 35 to 40 years or more if they are in safe surroundings. The public are fascinated at the appearance of zebras. Children and adults do not ride on the backs of zebras. However, children and adults ride on the backs of horses. Zebras are admired for their unusual, beautiful stripes.

FORTY-SEVEN

Danielle The Seamstress

Danielle Parks was taught to sew by her mother while she was growing up. She learned to darn clothing. Then she learned to sew seams. Her mother taught Danielle to use a sewing machine. She learned to cut out dress patterns. She sewed the patterns to make different dresses. Then she learned to cut out patterns for skirts and blouses. Eventually, Danielle learned to knit and crochet.

As Danielle grew up she became a very good seamstress. She majored in Home Economics in high school. She took sewing classes while she was in high school. As a result, she decided to become a professional seamstress once she graduated from high school. She worked in a clothing factory first. She was instructed to sew different patterns used in the factory.

Five years went by. So Danielle had a lot of experience working in a sewing factory. Finally, Danielle decided to open her own seamstress shop. She had to pay rent every month. The rent was $1,500 a month. Danielle had to purchase sewing machine, fabric materials, thread and sewing patterns. She opened her sewing business as soon as she had enough sewing equipment and sewing materials.

Danielle was able to keep her private seamstress business open because her sewing business continued to increase. She developed a very good reputation as a seamstress. Her parents were very proud of their daughters' success as a seamstress.

In time, Danielle opened more seamstress businesses in different locations. She hired other seamstresses to work in these new businesses. More and more customers had clothes sewn. Wedding dresses, maids of honor dresses and men's dress suits continued to be sewn from scratch.

Danielle's expanded business helped her to prosper. She developed brand names which people valued. She became wealthy from her expanded seamstress business. She was known for sewing fancy buttons on blouses, suits and dresses to add to their artistic designs.

Danielle eventually got married to someone who accepted her ambitions as a seamstress and owner of different seamstress businesses. Danielle gave birth to four children. She continued to work even when she was pregnant with each child. When her four children grew up they worked at different seamstress shops. Danielle appointed her children to important roles such as managers and head seamstresses. When Danielle passed away she had left a will stating that her four children would inherit the seamstress businesses. She left her children with successful seamstress businesses so they would prosper.

FORTY-EIGHT

The Vegetarian Banquets

Hindus and Rosicrucians usually are vegetarians. They eat vegetables, fruits, nuts, grains, legumes, beans and some dairy products. Some of them are vegans. Vegans do not eat any dairy products.

Rosicrucians put on lavish vegetarian banquets in Oceanside, California and in San Jose, California. A wide variety of vegetarian dishes, vegetables, fruits, nuts, breads, beans and desserts are arranged on a long banquet table. The table is covered with a beautiful, table cloth. There may be flower bouquets arranged on this long table.

Many salads are in bowls and large dishes in a special section. For instance, a red bean salad mixed with corn kernels, chopped celery, chopped green and red peppers with a special herb dressing is delicious. A chopped cabbage salad with chopped walnuts, chopped celery and shredded carrots was appetizing mixed with mayonnaise, vinegar, salt and pepper. A tossed, dark green lettuce salad with baby tomatoes, chopped carrots, green peppers, chopped green and black olives, chopped celery mixed with chopped fish, basil and parsley with an herbal dressing tastes very good.

Pasta dishes with steamed noodles mixed with a tomato cheese sauce with basil, thyme, salt and pepper is delicious. Lasagna made with layers of pasta filled with red tomato and cheese sauce spread between the pasta layers with veggie burger, salt and pepper topped with basil and oregano is very delectable. Sauerkraut with chopped soya bean wieners is another interesting dish.

Mixed fruit salad is magnificent with cut strawberries, pineapple, pears, tangerines, apples and raisins which is mouth watering. Cut peaches with raspberries and raisins is another tasty dish. Lemon meringue pie made with egg whites and a lemon filing is poured in a pie crust. Lemon meringue is rimmed with a whipped white egg filling which is baked until it becomes a light golden brown. Lemon meringue pie is a very tasty treat especially at a banquet. Other desserts on the banquet table are applesauce cake, scones, raisin bread cake, peach cobbler, cherry pie, blueberry cake and custard pudding.

Casserole dishes on the banquet table are zucchini with stewed tomatoes topped with chopped basil and oregano, potatoes au gratin, creamy corn with cooked green and red peppers, veggie burgers topped with chopped, cooked onions and tomato sauce, vegetarian burgers with lettuce, sliced tomatoes, pickles with mustard, soya bean steaks topped with chopped parsley and thyme, etc.

The vegetarian banquet looked magnificent. All the food was nutritional. There was home made rye bread, whole wheat bread, sesame seed bread and seven grain Ezekiel bread. All the vegetarian food was enjoyed at the Rosicrucian banquet. Vegetarian banquets are more delicious than regular banquets.

FORTY-NINE

Tango Dancing

Tango dancing became popular in South America in Rio de Janeiro and Buenos Aires. Tango dancing is a unique form of movement. Tango dancers swing from right to left as they tap and turn their feet and move their legs. Tango rhythm is syncopated. Long gliding steps and dips are performed.

In the movie FLYING DOWN TO RIO tango dancers performed at large dance halls. Ginger Rogers and Fred Astaire became a well known dance couple. They performed the tango in FLYING DOWN TO RIO. Tango dancing has existed since the 1920s. Many dancers have learned the tango.

Other couples who dance a lot usually perform tango dances. Orchestras play background, tango music. They wear attractive costumes when they perform the tango.

The tango will probably remain well known and popular especially in South America. Young adults and older adults will continue to learn how to dance the tango because this style of dancing is unique. Many people have learned to dance the tango.

Fiction

FIFTY

Walking Adventures

Jim Hawkins and Mary Lou Jensen both liked to walk long distances. They had known each other since First Grade. They were physically fit and willing to go on long walks across the country.

Jim was ready to take another walking spree. He was able to walk up into the hills to the Coastal Ranges. Jim invited Mary Lou to come with him. They packed their backpacks with clothes, camping supplies and food. Once they dressed in their walking clothes, which included walking boots, Jim and Mary Lou put their backpacks on and they started their walking adventures.

It was a pleasant day. The sun was out and there were few clouds. Jim and Mary Lou began walking from Pismo Beach in California where they lived. They headed east towards the Coastal Ranges which were approximately 42 miles away. They walked towards San Luis Obispo. They walked along Highway 101 until they could see the Coastal Ranges in the distance. Then they walked into a large open field of wild grass, wild flowers such as yellow sour grass and lupine. They continued walking towards the pink reflected Coastal ranges which stood out. They walked past cattle and some wild deer. They were grazing in the fields.

By late afternoon, Jim and Mary Lou had reached the foot of the Coastal Ranges. The sun was beginning to go over the horizon in the West. It was starting to get dark.

Mary Lou and Jim gathered loose limbs which they cut up and piled on the ground in a campfire hole. Jim lit the pile of limbs with a match. The campfire provided light and warmth. Mary Lou laid out bedrolls on the ground. She unpacked food from the backpacks. Mary Lou prepared hamburger patties. She used a frying pan to fry the hamburger patties. While the meat was cooking, Mary Lou sliced up potatoes, carrots, celery and green peppers and she steamed them in a cooking pot over the campfire. She toasted hamburger buns. Then she spread mustard on the hamburger buns. The hamburger patties were fried and ready to place on the toasted buns.

It was time to eat once the potatoes and vegetables had been boiled. Jim and Mary Lou sat on a canvas tarp which was laid out on the ground. Jim and Mary Lou ate their hamburgers and steamed potatoes and vegetables. For dessert they each ate an apple. They sipped herb tea stored in thermo bottles.

After their meal, Jim and Mary Lou set up two tents. Jim pitched some wood stakes in the ground. Canvas tents were pulled up with ropes and tied to hold them up. The bedrolls were placed in the tents. Jim and Mary Lou sipped their tea near the campfire. They watched the Moon come up. The Moon was very bright as it moved slowly across the night sky. The stars came up and sparkled in the sky. Mary Lou and Jim had become close friends through the years. This was one of their many adventures.

That night Jim and Mary Lou went into their tents to sleep. During the night it rained. The campfire went out because of the pouring rain. Jim and Mary Lou remained in their tents so they wouldn't get wet. The next morning it had stopped raining. Jim gathered twigs and pieces of loose wood. He rebuilt a new fire.

Mary Lou fried scrambled eggs, bacon and sliced potatoes in different skillets with canola oil. She put salt and pepper on the eggs and potatoes. She fried bacon and toasted whole wheat bread. It was time to eat breakfast. Mary Lou made hot coffee as well. Jim and Mary Lou ate their breakfast. Then they took the tents down and rolled them up. They cleaned up the dishes and cleaned the campsite area. Jim made sure the campfire was out. He poured rainwater over the embers in the campfires.

Jim and Mary Lou put their backpacks on and they began walking up the mountain. They had to climb up slopes and cross crevices. It got steeper and steeper as they climbed up the Coastal Ranges. It became warmer and warmer as they climbed higher and higher. They took off their jackets and continued to feel the warmth of the sun.

Cecelia Frances Page

By mid morning Jim and Mary Lou had climbed almost to the top of the mountain range. They saw squirrels in holes. Wild horses were scurrying around in scrubs in open crevices. Wild flowers were blooming on the slopes. Some of the wild flowers were fragrant.

Jim and Mary Lou reached the top of the last slope by late morning. They had managed to climb steep slopes and step onto ledges on the way up the mountain. They were able to see a spectacular view for many miles. They witnessed fertile, green valleys below. They were able to see the ocean in the distance near the horizon. They took photographs of the magnificent view.

After resting and enjoying the view Jim and Mary Lou started down the mountain slopes. They used ropes and pulleys in order to go down the mountain. It took three and a half hours to reach the bottom of the mountain. Jim and Mary Lou needed to rest. They were sweating and weary. They decided to set up a campsite at the foot of the mountain range. They cooked a meal and ate more food. Then they put up their tents. They watched the sunset with its vivid colors of orange, yellow, red and purple. Then the Moon came out again. The stars sparkled in the night sky. They saw the Big Dipper, the Bear and Pleiades constellations. They were fascinated with the night sky.

The next morning Jim and Mary Lou began walking back to Pismo Beach after breakfast. They had cleaned up their camp. They saw spotted owls, squirrels, meadowlarks, sparrows, some robins and quails as they continued walking across the meadows and fields to the highway. They saw a few deer grazing in the distance.

Jim and Mary Lou continued walking until they came back to Pismo Beach. Their feet were tired. They had sores on their feet because they had walked a long time. They were glad to be back in Pismo Beach where they lived. They rested for a month before they went on another walking adventure.

Fiction

FIFTY-ONE

The Blessed Trinity

Kala Moreland lived in a fairyland in an enchanted land of mystery 1,000 years before Christ. Kala often walked into enchanted forests and lit up caves. She found sparkling gemstones which fascinated her. She carried some gemstones in her pocket for good luck charms.

Kala tried not to be superstitious. She believed shadows over the Moon and Sun meant something terrible would happen. She believed that black cats brought bad luck. She also believed that shattered mirrors brought bad luck. Kala wanted to believe in the wisdom of different sages. She believed in gods and goddesses, fairies and angels.

One day when Kala was walking in an enchanted forest she heard some unusual sounds. Celestial fairies suddenly appeared near Kala. They were beaming with light as they fluttered around in the air through the trees. They were singing harmonious melodies as they flew around. Kala observed twelve fairies moving near her.

Suddenly, a very bright ray of white light flashed down through the trees over Kala's head. This light flooded Kala's body and aura. She felt transformed by this white light. She felt at peace and she realized some divine being was sending her this pure, white light. Kala felt serene and safe in this enchanted forest.

The fairies continued to sing their celestial songs. Then some angels appeared before Kala. They radiated with white light. They looked at Kala with pure, peaceful expressions. Kala continued to feel completely peaceful. She felt that she had risen into a higher plane or dimension. She spoke to the angels, who wore white gowns and golden slippers.

Kala asked, "Who are you?" One of the angels said with a sweet, angelic voice, "We are angels of healing and mercy." Kala asked, "Why are you here?" Another angel replied sweetly." We have come to bless you and heal you." Kala thought about what these angels said to her. The angels moved around Kala showering her with radiant, healing light. She felt completely healed of any possible affirmatives and maladies.

A divine being appeared before Kala. This divine being radiated pure love, harmony, balance as well as pure white light. Kala noticed the divine being had golden long hair, purple-blue eyes and wore a robe of pure white light with gleaming gold strands in His robe. He wore white and gold slippers. This divine being wore a radiant medallion around his neck. Within the medallion Kala could see a gold key with three diamond stones which were blazing with sparkling light.

This magnificent, divine being spoke very gently and tenderly to Kala. He said, "You have entered a higher dimension of creation. We live in peace and harmony here. We are One with all life here. You have the opportunity to dwell among us for awhile. You will learn how and why we live on a higher plane of consciousness. Come with me child of divine calling. I will escort you through our higher kingdom of divinity."

Kala walked with the divine being who was called Divine One. He showed her divine gardens with purple, gold, pink, yellow and white, etheric flowers with spiral pedals. Kala witnessed golden plumed, etheric birds. She walked on a golden pathway of light. Kala felt she was in a heavenly abode. She felt very happy and blissful.

The Divine One took Kala to a white, etheric temple which had pillars of white and gold. They came to a central altar. Kala saw a golden cross, a golden key and a golden stone on this sacred altar. Kala was mystified by these sacred treasures. The Divine One said, "Behold, the blessed trinity of love, will and wisdom.

The Divine One kneeled before the sacred altar. Kala decided to kneel before this magnificent altar. She heard a pure, serene voice speak. "You have come to the sacred altar of divinity. I AM within you always. I bring you love, peace, harmony, balance and Oneness. Live in peace, love and harmony wherever you go. Remember, I Am with you always." Kala was showered with more radiant, white light by the Divine One.

When Kala returned to the enchanted forest she was sealed with white light. She continued to dwell there in peace, harmony, love and balance. She had been transformed forever. She lived by the blessed trinity of love, will and wisdom.

Fiction

FIFTY-TWO

Romance During A Journey

Romantic feelings are very intimate and special. When a man and woman fall in love they feel especially good inside. There is a chemical and magnetic attraction that draws couples together. Mutual interests and hobbies bring couples close together such as dancing, music, tennis, golf, traveling, reading books, etc.

Maureen Graham traveled on a Greyhound bus around California. She sat alone part of the time. Sometimes, Maureen sat near other passengers. She visited with different passengers who sat next to her. She sat by the window often so she could enjoy the scenery as she traveled in the Greyhound bus.

Maureen traveled from San Diego to Eureka, California. The Greyhound stopped at different Greyhound stations to pick up more passengers. Maureen met a lot of people while she traveled around California. After she had traveled for seven days and six nights a male passenger, Mark Sheldon, who was 36 years old, sat next to Maureen. He was handsome with black hair, blue eyes and he was well built. Maureen was 32 years old. She was 5 foot 6 inches in height. She was stocky and strong. She had strawberry blonde hair and hazel eyes. She was attractive in her own way.

Mark was open and friendly to Maureen. He began talking about his travels around America and Europe. Maureen listened to Mark's description of his travels to different interesting places. Mark was an interesting conversationalist while he traveled next to Maureen. Maureen noticed that Mark was not wearing a wedding band on his left, fourth finger.

The bus driver continued to travel north on Highway 101 towards Los Angeles. It would take at least three hours for the bus to arrive in Los Angeles at the L.A. Greyhound Station. So, Mark and Maureen had plenty of time to become acquainted. Mark talked about his childhood days. He said he grew up in Palm Springs in California. He enjoyed school and participated in sports such as basketball, hockey, tennis and baseball. He said he excelled in academic subjects. He liked to read and write. He had written over 100 poems.

Maureen listened quietly as Mark continued to talk about himself. She was fascinated with his description of his childhood days. She enjoyed listening to his interest in poetry especially. She hoped he would be able to recite some of his original poems. Mark continued to talk about his poetry writing.

Time went by while the Greyhound bus moved along. Mark kept talking to Maureen. Finally, he asked Maureen about her life. Maureen started talking about herself. She said she grew up in Atascadero, California. She mentioned that there was a zoo in Atascadero. She said she worked at the Atascadero Zoo full time. She liked to take care of the zoo animals. She fed most of the animals and cleaned out their cages. She especially enjoyed petting zebras, goats and sheep. She fed raw fruit to the monkeys, apes and tropical birds. She fed barley, hay and oats to the goats, zebras, sheep and gazelles. Meat was fed to the lions, tigers and panthers. There were a flock of pink flamingos near a manmade pond. There were roosters and chickens fenced in a special place.

Mark listened intently to Maureen as she spoke about her life. He found out that she liked to travel, play tennis, golf and volleyball. Maureen liked to read and she wrote short stories and novels. Mark looked at Maureen warmly. He noticed her eyes sparkled when she looked at him.

The Greyhound bus stopped in Los Angeles at the Greyhound Station. Mark and Maureen stepped out of the bus. It was lunch time. Everyone had two hours to relax and enjoy a break before the bus continued on its scheduled route. Mark asked Maureen to join him for lunch. She accepted his invitation. They walked out of the L.A. Greyhound Station and went down the street until they came to a café which served a variety of food such as Mexican, American and Italian dishes.

Mark and Maureen sat at a window table. They were given menus to look at. Mark decided to order fish and chips with a green salad. Maureen ordered veal cutlet with mashed potatoes, veggies, clam chowder and garlic bread. They ordered herbal mint hot tea. The café was nicely decorated with colorful paintings. The tables had checker-colored table cloths with a bouquet of daisies and tulips on each table. The café was filled with customers.

Maureen and Mark glanced around while they sipped mint tea and waited for their food. The server served a green salad to Mark and clam chowder to Maureen. Maureen told Mark that she had lived in Los Angeles for five years while she attended UCLA. She told Mark that she had majored in English and minored in Sociology. When she finished her college training she had looked for a job as an English teacher. She told Mark that she substituted for nearly a year while she was looking for a full time job as an English teacher. However, there were no, fulltime English jobs available because the budget had been cut in California. So, Maureen went back to Atascadero and eventually got a job as a zookeeper. She said the pay was not much, but she enjoyed working at the zoo.

The main course was brought to Mark and Maureen's table. They began eating their lunch. Mark talked about his present life. He said he had attended Harvard University back East. Maureen asked, "What did you major in?" Mark mentioned, "Law and Social Science. I became a lawyer." Maureen was impressed. Mark continued, "I have been a lawyer for 10 years." Maureen asked, "Where do you live?" Mark answered, "I live in Ojai, California.

Maureen was glad Ojai is an interesting place. Mark continued, "I have lived in Ojai for 10 years. I practice law there. Maybe you can come to visit me in Ojai someday." Maureen's eyes lit up. She sensed that Mark really liked her. She smiled warmly at him. They continued to eat their lunch.

After lunch, Mark and Maureen walked around for awhile. They came to a nearby park. They saw a variety of trees, verdant-green grass and flowers such as daisies, lilacs, tulips and some azaleas. The park was quite colorful and beautiful. Mark and Maureen sat on a park bench under a large magnolia tree. They saw white magnolia flowers on this tree. There was shade under the magnolia tree.

Mark said, "I am glad I met you on the bus. Let's continue to sit together until this trip is over." Maureen responded warmly. "Wonderful. We will have an opportunity to become more acquainted. I am glad I met you, too." Mark and Maureen returned to the L.A. Greyhound Station. It was time to board the bus. They sat together.

The Greyhound bus driver continued his route to Santa Barbara. He drove close to the ocean. Mark and Maureen were able to see scenic views of the Pacific Ocean. There was a lot of light blazing near the horizon. The ocean sparkled in the sunlight. Mark and Maureen continued to visit during their journey. The bus arrived in Santa Barbara by 5:15 p.m.

All the passengers stepped out of the bus. The journey would continue the next morning. The passengers would have to find a motel or hotel to stay in overnight. Mark and Maureen decided to stay in the same hotel. They went to the California Hotel near the ocean on State Street in Santa Barbara. They took a taxi downtown once they had arranged to stay at the hotel.

Once Mark and Maureen were downtown they stepped out of the taxi and they walked around downtown. There were a variety of restaurants, cafes and shops. Mark and Maureen browsed around in different shops which displayed ceramics, pottery, jewelry and clothes, etc. They had fun browsing around. Maureen found an attractive dress which she tried on. Mark found some colorful ties and several interesting shirts.

Maureen and Mark selected a Mexican restaurant downtown near State Street to eat dinner. The Mexican restaurant was decorated with serapes, Mexican hats and pottery as well as paintings of Mexico. Mexican music was playing. They selected combination dinners with cheese and beef enchiladas, tamales, tacos, rice and beans. The Mexican food was good and filling. Guacamole and sour cream was served as toppings on the beans and tacos. The Mexican food was sumptuous. Mark ordered a non-alcoholic, O'Douls beer. Maureen had lemonade.

After dinner, Mark and Maureen strolled around on State Street. Lights were lit up near the street. Mark and Maureen came to a large patio with large clay pots with colorful flowers. There were patio tables and chairs up and down the patio corridor. They sat at a patio table and had some Cappuccino coffee. They watched people passing by as they drank their Cappuccino.

Mark and Maureen decided to go down to the beach. They walked down to the beach from the California Hotel, which was near the beach. They walked on the beach near the ocean. The sand was smooth and partially warm. The ocean was a deep blue. Waves splashed to shore. Mark and Maureen enjoyed walking barefoot in wet beach sand. They were able to relax and observe seagulls, pelicans and sandpipers on the beach, in the ocean and in the sky.

It became dark and the Moon came out over the ocean. The Moon was large, bright and round. Mark and Maureen observed the Moon. Mark held Maureen's hand as they walked on the beach. Mark decided to kiss Maureen on the mouth. He kissed her tenderly. She responded to his kiss. He kissed her again under the moonlight. This romantic setting was a special place for Mark and Maureen to embrace.

When Mark and Maureen went back to the California Hotel, Mark kissed Maureen again near her hotel room. Maureen didn't invite Mark into her hotel room because she didn't want to be too easy to make love to. Mark didn't try to tempt Maureen to have sex that night. He behaved like a gentleman. Maureen thought about Mark that night. She wondered what it would be like to be intimate with Mark.

Maureen had been intimate with different men who left her in the past. She was 32 years old and she had never been married. She hoped to be asked to be married. She thought about Mark as someone who might want to marry her.

The next day the Greyhound bus tour continued. Mark and Maureen sat together on the bus. The tour continued from Santa Barbara north on Highway 101 towards Goleta, then Los Alamos, Santa Maria, Arroyo Grande, Pismo Beach, San Luis Obispo, Morro Bay, Cambria, King City, San Jose and San Francisco. The passengers stayed over night in motels in Morro Bay and San Francisco. Mark and Maureen ate out together and went to some interesting events in Cambria, San Jose and San Francisco. They had a wonderful time on this tour along the coast of California.

Maureen had fallen in love with Mark. They experienced many romantic moments along their tour in California. When the Greyhound tour was over, Mark came to Atascadero to see Maureen. She showed him around especially at the Atascadero Zoo. Mark met Maureen's parents. He brought his car. He was able to drive her to Ojai in a few days. Mark took Maureen to several gourmet restaurants in Ojai.

He took her to a pottery shop, an art gallery and to a Metaphysical Center while she was in Ojai. After becoming well acquainted with Maureen, Mark eventually asked Maureen to marry him. She accepted Mark's proposal enthusiastically. Mark and Maureen were married in Ojai a year later. They were happy together.

Fiction

FIFTY-THREE

Felicity Met Alex In The Fourth Dimension

Felicity Martin lived in a time when souls were freer to become aware of deeper metaphysical truths and interior reality. Felicity was open and eager to find out as much as she could about other dimensions. She had grown up in a metaphysical center on the Central Coast of California.

Felicity had learned about metaphysical truths such as the laws of centralization and karma known as cause and effect, polarities known as opposites of positive and negative and transmutation. She became aware of the trinity of love, will and wisdom as well.

Day by day Felicity continued to become aware of God Reality and inner truths. She expanded her consciousness and became enlightened. She came in contact with other enlightened individuals who were aware of metaphysical truths. She sat among Buddhists, Theosophists, Rosicrucian's and Hindus to meditate quietly.

Felicity often sat out in beautiful, peaceful meadows to experience peaceful awareness. She often lifted her consciousness while she meditated. Step by step she raised her consciousness and visualizations to the fourth dimension. In the fourth dimension Felicity experienced more peace, light, wisdom and spiritual beauty and consciousness. She experienced bliss and tranquility in this higher dimension.

While Felicity raised her consciousness to the fourth dimension she encountered experiences with spirit beings who dwelled there. Some of the spirit beings communicated with Felicity. They communicated blissful messages about the wonders in the fourth dimension. One spirit being came over to Felicity and said, "Welcome to our higher dimension. You will experience peace, joy and oneness here. We exist in Nirvana." Felicity felt a oneness with this spirit being. She wanted to remain in this higher dimension of reality.

Then Felicity came to a crystal, sparkling river where she bathed in a mystical light which permeated her whole being. She was renewed by the pure substance in the crystal river. While she was bathing in this crystal river she saw another being who was also bathing in the white light in the crystal river. He came close to her and spoke to her. This being had blonde hair, clear blue eyes and he wore a white robe and his feet were uncovered. He continued to bathe near Felicity.

Felicity continued to bathe in the crystal river. This being spoke to Felicity. He said, "My name is Alex. I am glad you are here. I bathe here often. You must be a new comer because I haven't seen you here before." Felicity replied, "Yes, I haven't been to this crystal river before. The white light and pure magnetic effect has a healing effect. I am pleased to be here. I hope to be able to come here again and again. How often have you been here?" Alex answered, "I have been to this crystal river many times. There are many wonders and spiritual opportunities in this higher dimension. If you continue to come here you will continue to raise your consciousness and you will experience balance, equilibrium, harmony, divine love and wisdom."

Felicity and Alex continued to bathe in the crystal river in order to purify their four lower bodies of dross and darkness. They experienced inner peace and tranquility. Felicity hoped to meet Alex in the fourth dimension again in the future.

Nonfiction

FIFTY-FOUR

Intergalactic Experiences

We have entered into an intergalactic age. We can learn from outer and inner space experiences and travels. There are many dimensions in the Cosmos. Parallel planes exist which effect one another. Parallel planes may be similar to one another.

Intergalactic awareness exists in the Cosmos. We are limited in how far we can travel in our galaxy. Astronauts have traveled only in our solar system. However, there are many galaxies in our Universe. Each galaxy has millions of solar systems. Each solar system spirals around within its own galaxy.

Galaxies move around in spiral motion around the Cosmos. Solar systems are still being created in different galaxies. We should learn all we can about our Universe. Astronomers are looking through well developed telescopes to study outer space. Galaxies have been discovered in outer space by astronomers.

We should accept that there is intelligent life in outer space. UFOs have been seen coming to Earth for many centuries. There are flying saucers, cigar shaped UFOs and cylinder shaped UFOs, etc. Different space beings have been seen on Earth. About twelve types of beings have been seen.

Humanity should learn to be receptive to outer space beings. We can learn to communicate effectively with other intelligent beings if we remain open minded and learn all we can about life on other planets.

FIFTY-FIVE

Snow Country

Snow country may be very cold during winter months and in late Autumn and early Spring. Snow falls quite frequently, covering the ground, roofs on buildings and onto trees and other plants. Snow is very interesting to look at, especially when snow flakes can be seen with geometric designs.

Snow fills up in valleys, meadows and mountains. Doorsteps and doorways are piled up with snow after a snow storm. Snow has to be shoveled away from doorways so occupants can open doors and be able to step outside.

Snow usually remains on the ground when it is very cold outside and the sun is not shining. Eventually the snow melts and becomes water. Then it evaporates in time and disappears. More snow falls and the cycle begins again.

Snow may become thick once it keeps falling over and over. In cities in upper North America and in the East it snows during the late Autumn, Winter and early Spring. The streets and sidewalks are filled with snow. The sidewalks become wet and slippery. Snow must be shoveled off the sidewalks and out of the streets.

People who live in snow country must become used to sluggish snow in pathways, on sidewalks and in doorways. Cars usually have chains put on them because the streets are slippery.

Everyone wears warm clothing such as woolen sweaters, coats and head scarves and neck scarves as well as warm turtle neck sweaters, warm pants and socks. Leather boots keep one's feet and legs warm. Thick woolen, winter clothing is necessary especially in severe, cold weather when it snows and rains.

Snow country is the place to go skiing and tobogganing on bobsleds. Ice forms in puddles and lakes. Ice skating is popular in winter months as well. Skiing is enjoyed up in high hills and mountain slopes.

Snowballs are made and thrown back and forth outdoors in snow country. Snowmen and snowwomen are created outdoors for passer bys to enjoy. Snow can be used to make snow cones. Different flavors are poured over the snow cones. Snow cones taste good.

Snow exists and settles usually in Alaska, Canada, Northern America, Greenland, Iceland, Antarctica, parts of South America, Europe and Russia especially during Winter months. The snow eventually melts and melted snow on the mountains flows down as springs. This pure spring water is used for many people as drinking water. Snow is a valuable resource because it is used by many people. Snow country exists because severe cold weather turns rain into snow which falls as snowflakes.

Fiction

FIFTY-SIX

The Journalist

Marty Felderhauser took Journalism in high school and college. He learned to write factual articles, feature stories, sports articles and editorial columns. He became a very good writer. He kept writing articles for the high school newspaper and college newspaper. He was successful in Journalism.

So, Marty became a journalist. He applied for jobs at different local newspapers. Finally, he was able to receive a journalism position in a city twenty-five miles from where he lived. He was glad to have a full time job as a journalist.

The senior editor of the newspaper assigned Marty to different writing assignments. Marty was asked to write factual articles only when he began as a journalist for the newspaper. He gathered local events and happenings referring to what, why, where, how and who as he wrote factual articles. The senior editor began to assign Marty to feature stories after he had worked for the newspaper six months.

Marty interviewed important people in the city where he worked. He interviewed political leaders, teachers, celebrities and other interesting individuals. He interviewed the Mayor who was known as Mayor Todd Silverman. Marty asked Mayor Silverman, "Why did you want to become the Mayor of this city?" The Mayor replied, "I wanted to become Mayor in order to make positive and necessary changes in this city." Marty asked. "What changes do you want to make?" Mayor Silverman answered, "I want to improve the streets and some public buildings. The financial budget needs to be improved. I will have to collect more taxes in order to make these changes. This city should look better. With the streets improved it will be safer to drive vehicles such as cars, trucks and vans. Taxis can travel around better, too. Many buildings need to be repaired and repainted."

Marty continued to interview Mayor Silverman. He found out what new policies, bills and laws were being promoted in Mayor Silverman's administration. Marty wrote a feature story about Mayor Silverman's life and career in politics.

The next newspaper article was about teacher of the year. Marty went to the local high school to interview Michael Coleman who taught high school Biology and Physics. Mr. Coleman was very popular because he was a dynamic speaker; plus he had a sense of humor. Mr. Coleman used visual aids and he decorated his classroom with colorful, educational bulletin boards. Mr. Coleman maintained a very good relationship with his students. He stimulated his students to participate in class discussions. Mr. Coleman encouraged all his students to express themselves. He encouraged his students to complete their classroom assignments and homework. Most of his students did well in his classes. He was awarded a gold ribbon as best teacher of the year. Marty wrote an interesting feature story about Michael Coleman which was put on the front page of the local newspaper.

Marty Felderhauser worked at the local newspaper for ten years. He had a lot of experience writing a variety of different newspaper articles. Marty was offered a position as an overseas journalist. He accepted this journalist position. He traveled to Iraq to Baghdad as a reporter. He was willing to risk his life in Iraq.

Marty stayed at a hotel in Baghdad in Iraq. He heard bombing sounds. Some of the bombs were close to his hotel. Marty hoped he wouldn't be injured and killed in Iraq. He was assigned to report about the war in Iraq. He gathered reports about the Iraqi people and their struggle to become independent. A democratic government was being formed. The Iraqi people were given the opportunity to vote. However, when they went to vote they had to be careful so they wouldn't be shot by Al Qaeda. The streets of Baghdad were dangerous to walk in. Iraqi people even experienced attacks in their homes, especially if they defended American soldiers and supported them.

Marty walked in the streets of Baghdad to find out what he could during the daytime. He found out what was happening around Baghdad. He sent reports back to American newspapers about what was happening in Baghdad and surrounding areas in Iraq. He stayed in Iraq for several months.

The day before Marty was to return to America he was resting in his hotel. Suddenly his hotel was bombed. Everyone in this hotel was killed including Marty Felderhauser. His life on Earth was over.

Fiction

FIFTY-SEVEN

Traveling Adventures

Molly Brothers enjoyed traveling whenever she had some free time. She was an elementary school teacher. She had two and a half months off each summer. During this time she traveled to different places.

Each summer Molly traveled to some very interesting places. One summer she traveled to Australia and the Fiji Islands. She went to Sydney, the largest city in Australia. Sydney was clean and beautiful with red title roofs. The Australian people were friendly and healthy looking. She went to museums, art galleries and the famous Sydney Opera House and cultural events in Sydney.

Molly traveled to Ayers Rock which is the largest inland rock in Australia. Ayers Rock changed colors as the sun moved across the sky. This rock appears orange-red, then deep, dark red. Shadows appear at Ayers Rock from a distance in the afternoon. Molly met Aborigines near Ayers Rock. They lived near Ayers Rock. There were ancient Aborigine drawings and paintings on the Ayers Rock which go back thousands of years. Primitive drawings of Aborigine people and animals could be seen on the rock.

Molly was fascinated with Ayers Rock and the primitive Aborigine drawings and paintings. She saw wild Dingo dogs wandering around near Ayers Rock. They were looking for food. Molly avoided the Dingoes because they had sharp teeth. Molly stayed in a trailer near Ayers Rock for several days so she could enjoy Ayers Rock at different times of the day.

After several days Molly traveled to Queensland to Brisbane, Red Cliff and Scarborough which are near the ocean. She stayed over night in Brisbane. During the day Molly walked on the beach for miles. She went swimming in the ocean which was cold because it was winter in Australia in June. Molly tried to get used to the cold ocean water. She ran into the ocean and ran back out because of the cold water. She decided to lie on the beach sand so she could feel the sunlight on her body.

There were interesting restaurants in Brisbane. Fish and chips with cole slaw was a popular seafood dish. Molly put tartar sauce on her codfish. Her French fries were a golden brown. The cole slaw was also delicious. After lunch Molly went on a boat to Morton Island. On this island Molly went in a car around the island to see the scenery. There were fan palm trees, other tropical palm trees and pine trees, flowering trees and ferns. Morton Island was not populated.

Beaches on Morton Island stretched for miles. The turquoise ocean was magnificent. Molly shared a picnic lunch with other visitors who came to Morton Island. She ate a pastrami sandwich with lettuce, pickles and mustard on rye bread. Potato salad with eggs, cut, cooked potatoes sprinkled with chopped parsley, celery and pickles were served. Cut veggies such as carrots, green and red peppers, baby tomatoes and sliced broccoli and cauliflower were also served. Oatmeal cookies and chocolate cake were served for dessert with fresh, raw, cut fruit such as mangos, bananas and pineapple. Molly drank cool lemonade with her picnic lunch.

After lunch Molly and other visitors explored the pristine beach. Molly observed many crabs crawling on the warm, sandy beach. Seagulls, cormorants and pelicans were flying around in flocks. Many of the seabirds landed on the beach to rest and sun themselves.

Molly attended nightly entertainment in Brisbane. Guitar players, vocal soloists and dancers entertained audiences. Many tourists were visiting and vacationing in Brisbane. Australian folk songs were sung by the entertainers. The audience was given an opportunity to dance when a band played dance music. Molly was asked to dance. She danced with several Australian men. She was attractive with red hair, blue eyes and had a nice looking figure. Molly danced for hours and she had a wonderful time. Several Aussie men kept pursuing her.

Molly was 26 years old and she still was single. She had an opportunity to meet single, eligible men. She was happy to meet these Aussie men with their charming mannerisms and Australian accent. Molly met an Aussie man called Albert. Albert kept asking Molly to dance. He was tall, husky with light brown hair and brown eyes. He had prominent, facial features.

Molly was attracted to Albert. He was a good, dancing partner. He knew how to perform waltzes, jitter bug and tango dance. Molly was able to respond as a dancing partner. She had learned how to participate in folk dancing and perform modern dances when she was in high school and college. Molly had become a graceful dancer.

When the dance hall closed at midnight Albert took Molly back to her hotel. He told her that he had a good time with her. Albert said, "I want to see you again." Molly replied, "I will be in Brisbane for several more days. Then I will be going to the island of Fiji. Albert appeared concerned that Molly would be leaving so soon. He said, "Perhaps I could go to Fiji with you."

Molly smiled at Albert. She said, "I hardly know you." Albert answered, "We can become more acquainted. I am due for a vacation. Let's spend the day together tomorrow." Molly decided to spend the next day with Albert. They had breakfast together near Molly's hotel. After breakfast Albert took Molly sailing in the ocean at the Gold Coast which is south of the Brisbane Airport.

The adventure of sailing on Albert's catamaran was exciting for Molly. The ocean rippled up and down but the time finally came when Molly had to say goodbye to Albert. She knew he didn't want her to go so far away.

Molly and Albert went to Fiji together. They went by airplane near to Suva at the Fiji Airport, They registered at the hotel in Suva in separate hotel rooms. They walked up and down the main streets of Suva to enjoy the shops, cafes, art galleries, etc. They saw Hindu women dressed in Indian saris. Molly and Albert tasted Indian food at an Indian restaurant. They had curried lamb, curried rice, cut cucumbers, tomatoes and spicy pudding. Iced herb tea was served with the meal,

Albert rented a car and drove Molly around the island of Fiji. Rich red, lava soil existed everywhere. They observed tropical vegetation and palm trees as well as wild tropical flowers which blossomed everywhere. Albert and Molly saw thatched roofed huts along the way. They stopped along the white, pristine beaches to walk near the turquoise, Indian Ocean. Molly and Albert swam in the warm ocean. When it became late afternoon they enjoyed observing a crimson sunset.

When Molly and Alberta had enjoyed several days on the Fiji Islands they went back to Brisbane in Australia. It was time for Molly to catch a plane to America.

Albert kissed Molly tenderly at the Brisbane Airport just before she stepped onto the airplane. She promised to email Albert. He told her that he would call her. Molly got on the airplane and departed for America. She felt sorry about leaving Albert to travel so far away. She hoped to see Albert again.

When Molly arrived in Boise, Idaho she took a taxi from the airport to her home. She checked her phone messages and email letters. Sure enough, Albert had called her and left a message on her voice box machine. He said he already missed her. He said he planned to visit her soon. He had to make arrangements to take time off from his job first. Molly was excited and elated because Albert was planning to come soon to see her in Idaho. She looked forward to her reunion with Albert.

Nonfiction

FIFTY-EIGHT

Reincarnation Exists

The law of reincarnation exists. We incarnate one lifetime after another with intervals of rest and evaluation in between lifetimes. Edgar Cayce, known as a sleeping prophet, interviewed over a thousand people. He went into a trance state and told them about their past lives. Each person revealed experiences and memories from previous embodiments.

Several people remembered detailed accountings from past lives. Edgar Cayce Foundation researched the locations and people who knew of individuals who fit the description of individuals who revealed past lives. Evidence of past life regressions were recorded and kept in files in Edgar Cayce's office. A book called *There Is A River,* by Thomas Sugrue, is about Cayce's research about reincarnation at Virginia Beach in Virginia. Edgar Cayce has become well known for his careful, thorough records about reincarnation.

David Wilcox, who has become aware of reincarnation, realized that he was Edgar Cayce in his previous embodiment. He looks like Edgar Cayce as a young man. His astrological chart dove-tails with Edgar Cayce's chart. David Wilcox has the same birth sign and rising sign. David Wilcox has written books and magazine messages about reincarnation.

Reincarnation exists and has been written about in ancient Bibles and other religious writings. Sumerians, Hindus and ancient Jews were aware of reincarnation. Jesus spoke about reincarnation, which he was quoted about in secret scrolls hidden in caves in Israel. These hidden scrolls have been discovered in the 1940s.

The Western Bible such as the King James version has had many passages eliminated by the Nicean Council in the Roman Empire in the Fourth Century. Scholars state that 52 books with Gospels and prophet's messages have been taken out of the Bible. These contain references to reincarnation and karma. Metaphysical students and scholars are revealing the truth about reincarnation today. Madame Helena Blavatsky, who established the Theosophical Society, wrote and spoke about the reality of reincarnation and karma. Godfrey Ray King, who established the Saint Germaine foundation, wrote and spoke about reincarnation and karma. Francia La Due, Guardian-In-Chief of The Temple of the People in Halcyon, CA93421, California, also wrote and spoke about reincarnation and karma. Mark and Elizabeth Prophet, leaders of The Summit Lighthouse also wrote and spoke about reincarnation and karma.

FIFTY-NINE

Training Elephants

Elephants have lived on the Earth for millions of years. They existed during the dinosaur age. Elephants have thick, tough skin. They are gray with long trunks. They are capable of using their trunks to carry heavy objects such as logs.

An elephant can be trained step by step to do work for its owner and trainer. First, an elephant is captured and put in a fenced in area. They are fed once they obey and carry out step by step directions. It takes a day by day disciplinary procedure for an elephant to learn to obey and to follow instructions. An elephant learns to pick up a heavy log and hold it with its strong, long trunk. Then an elephant is instructed to carry the log from where it picked it up to carry it to another location. For centuries, elephants have been loading the long heavy trunks of trees on freighters for export from Sri Lanka

Day by day an elephant learns to pick up different, heavy objects. It is rewarded with food and even petted and stroked when it obeys and follows through with its assigned work. Elephants carry human passengers from one place to another.

Once an elephant has been carefully trained to carry out certain instructions and tasks it is a valuable, hard worker. In India and Asia, elephants are considered to be valuable workers. Poachers should be stopped from killing elephants for their ivory tusks. There are less elephants on Earth today. Some have been sent to zoos. Other elephants may roam free in jungles and savannahs. Many elephants have been trained to work for mankind. They tend to live long lives and they have excellent memories.

SIXTY

Wonders In The World

There are many wonders in the world. In ancient times there were giant pyramids, statues of Greek, Roman, Egyptian and Sumerian gods. In Constantinople a giant statue of a warrior stood near the harbor to protect it. The Colossus of Rhodes statue was one of the Seven Wonders Of The Ancient World.

A giant gold statue of Zeus at Olympia stands erect in a famous Greek temple regarded as one of the Seven Wonders Of The Ancient World. Phidias, a sculptor in 433 B.C. created the incredible statue of Zeus, known as king of the Greek gods. This statue was a gigantic 33 feet tall. It was made of ivory and gold. The Parthenon in Greece is another wonder of the world. The Greeks and Romans were excellent architects with the use of stones.

The Egyptians built enormous statues in Karnak in their temples and in front of their temples which are considered to be wonders. Their Egyptians boats were made out of papyrus and reeds. Egyptian boats were used to travel thousands of miles. The Egyptians were seafarers for many, many years.

The Amazon River is the longest river in the world. It has clean, purer water which can be used to drink and cook with. Millions of tropical trees exist near the Amazon River. Many people depend on the Amazon River for water. The Amazon River is one of the wonders of the world.

The Sphinx in Egypt's desert outside of Cairo is another wonder of the world. The Sphinx was built near the Great Pyramid of Giza. It can be seen for miles in the desert. Some secret treasures and ancient knowledge are said to be hidden inside the Sphinx.

The ancient city of Petra in the desert of Jordan is another wonder in the world. The buildings are built into the mountainside. The buildings appear to be Mediterranean architecture. This unusual city was built out in an isolated area in the desert.

Giant stone statues are lined up facing the ocean close to the shore on Easter Island. These statues appear to be "gods" from outer space. The stone statues appear to be staring across the ocean as if they are waiting for something to happen. These giant stone statues are wonders of the world.

Stonehenge in England is another wonder of the world. Stonehenge is made of enormous stones which are in a circular formation. The symbol of Pi is shaped in the stones. Archaeologists wonder who built Stonehenge.

Crop circles are wonders in the world. Their designs are very unique. Crop circles are designed in farming areas in fields of crops. They can be seen from aerial views. It appears that celestial beings from outer space have mysteriously designed crop circles by beaming down with laser energy and other methods from their spaceships and orbs, etc.

Hiram Bingham, an American archaeologist, discovered the lost city of Machu Picchu in Peru in 1911. This stone built, ancient city is located in the Andes Mountains, which was built around 1450 by the Inca people. The buildings were accurately fitted together with stones without mortars. Machu Picchu was a religious center with a stepped temple. The Incas used one area of their city for studying the Sun and the stars. Terraces around the city were designed for growing crops. 10,000 people once lived in Machu Picchu. The city was built on top of a much more ancient city from a lost civilization. The older culture had more advanced engineering and left no records.

The Great Wall of China was built by Shi Huangdi, the first ruler of united China. Work began on the Great Wall of China in 220 BC to protect the ruler's country from invaders. The wall was built up to 18 feet wide. Tall watchtowers were used for signaling in order to pass messages to soldiers along the wall

Angkor Wat was once the capital of the Khmer Empire in Cambodia in the 12th century by King Surgavorman II. This wondrous ancient city was unknown to the West until 1861, when French naturalist, Henry Mouhat discovered it. Archaeologists later found a temple dedicated to the Hindu god Vishnu with many beautiful carvings, huge moats and reservoirs.

The Acropolis in Athens, Greece, stands 148 feet high and was the legendary home of the city's gods and kings. Acropolis means "City at the top." The most famous temple on the Acropolis is the Parthenon. It dates from 447 to 432 B.C.

Borobudur is the world's largest Buddhist temple on the Indonesian island of Java. It was built between AD 778 and 850. Borobudur is a pyramid-like structure reaching 103 feet at its highest point. The temple consists of a series of platforms, which represent stages in the life of a Buddhist. It includes over 500 figures of Buddha as well as bell-shaped shrines, each containing a statue.

Babylon became the largest city in ancient times, covering an area of up to 3.8 square miles. Babylon, the capital of a great empire, was situated on the Euphrates River about 55 miles south of Baghdad, near the modern town of Al-Hillah, Iraq. Babylon was famous for its architecture and as a center of learning and religion. At one time there were hanging gardens in Babylon which brought more of a natural, beautiful look to Babylon. Water may have been channeled to the gardens from the Euphrates River in a system of canals.

Some mighty monuments are the Statue of Liberty, New York Harbor, massive totem poles in Alaska, Trojan's marble columns in Rome, Italy, Crazy Horse Statue in the black Hills of South Dakota and Mount Rushmore in the Black Hills of South Dakota. Motherland is an enormous statue of 270 feet in Volograd, Russia.

Fiction

SIXTY-ONE

The Special Photographs

Murray Staten was a professional photographer. He had been taking photographs for many years as a hobby. He decided to become a professional photographer when he was 17 years old.

Murray had used a Kodak camera to take colored pictures. He also took black and white photographs. Murray collected hundreds of photographs. He put most of his photographs in photo albums. He labeled each photo. He was able to distinguish between photographs by classifying them into categories and specific topics.

Many of Murray's photographs were sent to magazines, newspapers and used in published books on front covers, back covers and in interior sections of books. Murray Staten became well known as a photographer. His photographs were exquisite and spectacular. He developed all his photographs in his photo studios.

As Murray looked through his photo albums he came across photographs which were especially exceptional because of the colors, lighting and details in these photographs. He decided to mount them and put them in beautiful frames to display in art galleries.

Ten of Murray Staten's best photographs were placed in art galleries around America and Europe. Reproductions were made of these ten photographs so that millions of people could purchase them. Murray had a photograph of a seascape with a magnificent sunset. Another photograph was of the Taj Mahal and gardens. A third photograph was of the Swiss Alps which had snow on them. A fourth photograph was a close up of a person dressed in a beautiful dress and fancy hairdo. Five more photographs were of magnificent landscapes such as the Grand Canyon, Ayers Rock and waterfalls such as Niagara Falls.

When millions of people bought reproductions of the ten photographs, Murray Staten received 60 percent of the royalties. He became very wealthy because of the success of his photographs that were sold.

Murray Staten used some of the money to purchase a photography school for adults. Many young adults attended Murray Staten's Art School. Murray became head of all the photography school. His students became professional photographers. Many of them displayed their photography in art galleries.

Murray Staten taught his students freelance photography and the use of perspective, lighting, shadows and color blends. Many of Murray's students became excellent photographers.

Fiction

SIXTY-TWO

The Enlightened Poet

Seana Shubert learned to write poetry when she was in high school. She had an English teacher who taught creative writing. Her English teacher read well known poems by great poets. She read poems by Henry Wadsworth Longfellow, Robert Frost, Emily Barrett Browning, Lord Tennyson, Lord Byron, Ralph Waldo Emerson, Edgar Allen Poe and more.

Because Seana Shubert was inspired by her English teacher she began writing original poems. She recorded her poems in a notebook. She kept track of her original poems. She wrote free verse, rhyming poems and Haiku poems. Seana submitted many of her poems to magazines. She eventually wrote several poetry books which were published. Her poetry books became well known.

As Seana continued writing nature and philosophical poems she became more and more enlightened. She wrote religious poems as well. Seana looked within for inner truths and wisdom. Her poems were expressions of her deeper awareness and feelings.

Seana joined several philosophical groups where she became more aware of metaphysical truths and knowledge. She became more adept in her awareness of interior realities. She met other poets when she joined poetry groups.

Seana presented her philosophy and nature poems at community events, at church and at school. Some of her poems were put in <u>WHO'S WHO</u> and <u>BEST POEMS OF THE YEAR IN AMERICA.</u>

SIXTY-THREE

Participating In An Orchestra

Orchestras are formed with a combination of string instruments, wind instruments, percussion instruments, harps and pianos. These instruments are played together in rhythm. A director uses a director's stick to keep exact rhythm.

String instruments are violins, violas, cellos, bass fiddle, guitars, ukuleles and harps. Wind instruments are clarinets, flutes, trumpets, saxophones, bassinet, French Horn oboes and trombones. Percussion instruments are tambourine, xylophone, drums, cymbals and castanets. Pianos are played with white and black keys. Strings are inside of pianos.

Every orchestra participant must know how to play his or her musical instrument well. Orchestra members must learn to keep exact timing as they play in an orchestra.

Names of well known orchestras are the Boston Pops Orchestra, Berlin Philharmonic Orchestra, London Symphony Orchestra San Francisco Orchestra, and Venice Orchestra. Some well known orchestra directors are Toscanini from Italy, David Levine from America, Leonard Bernstein from America and Yo Yo Ma from Hong Kong.

It is important for orchestra members to be on time for orchestra rehearsals. They are required to wear black suits with white shirts on stage during performances. They are required to follow the director's instructions and rhythm. Each orchestra member must know each orchestra piece which will be played in sequence.

Orchestras usually play background orchestra music for operas, operettas and stage plays. Orchestra music is still popular today. It may be used in films, VCR tapes and television programs. Firestone Television has presented orchestra performances. Carnegie Hall in New York City presents orchestra music. Orchestra music is needed for different music programs.

Fiction

SIXTY-FOUR

The Healing Spring

Priscilla Stillman was playing in a large meadow covered with grass and wild flowers such as lupin, yellow sour grass flowers and buttercups. Priscilla jumped up and down in this fragrant meadow. She saw butterflies which were yellow, white and multicolored. Bees were buzzing around wild flowers as they gathered pollen to take back to their beehives.

While the Sun was up in the sky, it was a bright, clear day. Priscilla continued to run about in the meadow freely. She finally rested by lying down in the grassy meadow to soak up the fresh air and to feel the warmth of the Sun. When Priscilla rested for awhile she decided to walk across the meadow to look around. She walked for several miles. She saw more grass and wild flowers.

Then, suddenly, Priscilla came to a blue spring of fresh, pure water. Priscilla was surprised to come to this spring. She decided to go into the spring to cool off. She stepped into the spring with her clothes off. There was no one else around when Priscilla went into the spring nude.

Priscilla had been drained of energy from her long walk through the meadow. When she went into the spring she felt completely recovered. Her vitality and energy returned. She realized that the spring water had healing power. She was glad to be restored with enough energy. She stayed in the spring for approximately 15 minutes. She finally stepped out of the refreshing spring.

After Priscilla put her clothes back on she walked through the meadow towards her home. She felt very energetic all the way back home. She wondered why she felt so good. Priscilla realized that she felt so much better after she had soaked in the spring.

This healing spring became well known in the region and then in England where Priscilla lived. Many needy people came to this healing spring to bathe so they could be healed of their maladies and diseases.

Nonfiction

SIXTY-FIVE

Historical Awareness About Greece

A golden age emerged in Greece after 479 BCE in Athens. In previous times the Minoans of Crete were the first to become artisans, architects and philosophers. In 1900 BCE, a wealthy Bronze Age civilization began on the island of Crete which lies about 75 miles from Greece at the southern end of the Aegean Sea.

A great Minoan civilization existed, which flourished for many hundreds of years until about 1300 BCE. The Minoans had a thriving economy based on trade. The Minoans exchanged goods with the Egyptians as well as people who lived on the eastern shores of the Mediterranean. This opened up the world of the Aegean to outside influences.

The Minoans built several large palaces, each with its own king. Knossos was one of three palaces, each with its own king. The royal palaces were very luxurious with colorful balconies and verandas. The Minoans had bathtubs and flushing toilets. Water for washing and drinking was fed through an elaborate system of pipes. Many rooms in the palace at Knossos were decorated with lavish wall paintings known as frescoes which describe a fascinating insight into Minoan life and religious worship. There were grand public areas and decorated apartments for the ruling elite.

One of the most notable achievements of the Minoan people was the development of two systems of writing. They used a form of hieroglyphs known as picture writing. Later, in about 1000 BCE, they developed a script known as Linear A, which was made up of signs and pictures. The writing was scratched onto clay tablets. Archaeologists believe these writings were a way of recording details of the food and other goods stored in the palace warehouses.

The decline of the Minoans may have started with a series of earthquakes or volcanic eruptions. By 450 BCE, the Minoan culture had collapsed and the palaces were destroyed. The Mycenaeans settled on mainland Greece about 2000 BCE. They were named after a place called Mycenal. The Mycenaeans lived in small, independent kingdoms, each based around a separate city. Mycenae was the richest and most powerful of these kingdoms.

The Mycenaean royal families lived in palaces, built around a large central room known as a megaron, which had a central hearth and a throne. The Mycenaean culture was one of fighting, raiding and hunting. After the conquest of Crete, the Mycenaeans became active traders throughout the Eastern Mediterranean. They traded with Egyptians.

The Mycenaeans adapted the writing systems of the Minoans and they devised their own script known as Linear B found at Knossos on Crete. Mycenaean script remained a mystery until 1952 when a young English man named Michael Ventris, managed to decipher the signs. He showed that Linear B represented an early form of Greek. The tablets contained mostly lists made by chariot-makers, carpenters, goldsmiths and weavers, recording details of exports such as furniture and cloth.

Mycenaean wealth is exposed by many archaeological finds from the palaces, including chairs and footstools, mirrors and musical instruments, stone lamps and ivory figures, bronze and large amounts of pottery. The tablets also tell us of the gods worshipped by the Mycenaeans. Religion was a central part of Greek life, even in early times.

The Greeks did not invent the alphabet. From the Middle East they improved the Phoenician system by adding letters to signify vowel sounds. In the process, they created the alphabet that is the ancestor of all European alphabets.

"The Greeks could not imagine a world without gods. They felt the presence of gods in their local streams and rivers and in their caves and mountains," stated Peter Ackroyd, a literary editor of the London SPECTATOR and book reviewer for THE TIMES in London. Athens, while Artemis, was the patron goddess of Ephesus.

According to the poets, the 12 most important gods lived at the top of Mount Olympus, the tallest mountain in Greece. These gods were known as the Olympians. Gods looked down on men and women, judging their behavior and influencing their lives from above. The Greeks believed the gods could take on human form and visit the Earth. Sometimes they fell in love with humans and even had children with them. Zeus, king of the gods, tried to keep their activities in check.

Important activities in Greek society games, theatrical events and celebrations were dedicated to a particular god or goddess. The Olympic Games were part of a festival dedicated to the god Zeus. These were pan-Hellenic (all-Greek) games which meant that athletes from all over Greece were allowed to take part. The Olympic Games were held every four years at the sanctuary of Zeus at Olympia, in western Greece. The games attracted athletes and spectators from all over the Greek world.

By the 7th Century BCE, the Greeks were becoming wealthy on trade. The cargoes exported on Greek ships included pots of perfume and ointment, large jars filled with wine and olive oil. Other exports included pottery and leather goods. They built with marble. The Greek cities imported grain and metals such as copper and iron.

As trade expanded the city-states continued to develop. Each city-state was governed by a group of wealthy aristocrats. These ruling groups were known as oligarchies. This means: "the rule of the few."

The two greatest forces in Greek history are Sparta and Athens. Sparta lay in a wide river valley cut off by mountains on either side. Sparta was founded in the 10th Century BCE by a group of people called Dorians, who had defeated the original inhabitants of the area. Sparta was formed from five neighboring villages. The territory of Sparta was very large, covering an area of 3,000 square miles.

The Spartans had very simple houses and no great public buildings. The Spartan mind and imagination were occupied only with matters of war and domination. All men had to serve in the army and their whole lives were dedicated to learning the art of battle.

The Spartans claimed to be the descendents of the children of the legendary hero Hercules. They conquered Laconia Laconia and Messenia. These conquests made Sparta one of the most powerful city-states of its time.

Spartan women had more freedom than women in other Greek cities. Young girls were educated from the age of seven. Like their brothers, they lived, slept and trained in barracks. They learned to read and write but most importantly they were trained from an early age in athletics, gymnastics and combat sports. At the age of 18, if a Spartan girl passed her fitness test, she was assigned a husband and allowed to return home. Spartan girls were regarded as the future mothers of a warrior breed. They were expected to stay in shape so that they would give birth to healthy sons who would grow up to be good soldiers.

Spartan women were much more independent than the women of other Greek city-states. They were allowed to own land and property. They didn't have to stay within their houses all the time. Spartan women sang and danced in front of men. They were brave and outspoken.

The state of Sparta was governed by two kings who ruled together equally. Five men known as ephors watched over the kings to ascertain that they obeyed their oaths of office. 30 men were elders. All other men had to be over 60 years of age. The council of elders acted as a supreme court of justice who drew up the laws and acted as judges.

In the middle of the 6th Century BCE, Sparta dominated most of the Peloponnese. It was the strongest military power in Greece. However, the population was steadily declining and the number of soldiers in the army decreased because of losing battles.

Sparta made a series of alliances with nearby states in the Peoponnese and formed a Peleponnesian League. Allie cities remained independent. Under Spartan leadership allied cities were protected. Sparta's rival was the city-state of Athens.

Chilon, an ephor ruler of Sparta in the 6th century BCE, was known as one of the 'Seven Wise Men of Greece' who won fame for his wise sayings.

Athens was the largest and most powerful of the Greek city-states. It was the center of Greek culture, famous for its art, drama, history and philosophy. Athens was located in central Greece. The Athenians lived beneath a hill called the Acropolis which means "high city". It was a fortified citadel where inhabitants took refuge when the city was under attack from hostile neighbors. Temples and sanctuaries were built in Athens.

Cecelia Frances Page

Athens was ruled by a group of rich aristocrats, who elected nine magistrates called archons to manage the affairs of the city. In about 632 BCE, an Athenian nobleman called Cylon attempted to set up a tyranny in Athens. Cylon was rejected by the Athenian people and his attempt to take over was unsuccessful. Cylon and his supporters were killed when they claimed sanctuary at the sacred altar of Athena.

The Athenians appointed a stern ruler called Draco. He created Athens' first written code of laws. In 594 BCE, an aristocrat named Solon was appointed Archon. Solon was a wise and just ruler. He tried to reform the state and set Athens on the path to democracy. His main goal was to establish good order among the people and to stop injustice in public life. He gave food to the poor, cancelled the debts of poverty-stricken farmers and developed a constitution (a system of government) that made wealth, not birth, the qualification for public office. He also abolished slavery as a punishment for getting into debt. He created a system of justice that allowed all citizens accused of a crime to appeal to a court of justice.

In the 6th Century BCE the emerging democracy of Athens was threatened by squabbling amongst the aristocratic families and this state was taken over by a tyrant called Peisistratus, who was a distant relative of Solon. Peisistratus turned out to be a wise and fair ruler. He increased trade with other countries and encouraged the planting of more trees. He introduced silver coins in Athens, stamped with the image of an owl, the symbol of Athena. Coinage was introduced in the 6th Century in place of bartering. The image stamped on the coins showed which city-state they were from indicating the financial strength of that area. The first coins were made of lumpus, a mixture of gold and silver. However, this was soon changed to silver.

Athens had state owned silver mines at Laurium in the south of Attica. Peisistratus began an ambitious program of public building in Athens. Athenian laborers were given work constructing new buildings. One of the most important buildings was a new temple to Athena on the Acropolis. This magnificent monument was adorned with various sculptures of limestone with a band of painted and sculpted decoration known as a frieze.

Greeks focused on order and symmetry in their Art and Architecture. Their hand made pottery was also exquisite. They made wine vessels, drinking cups and containers for Greek perfumed oils and ointments. Greek sculptors expressed human emotion and expression in their sculptures of human beings.

Under the rule of Peisistratus, Athens flourished and prospered. He had a large open market and meeting place erected close to the Acropolis. When Peisistratus died in 527 BCE, his two sons, Hippias and Hipparchus took over the government of Athens and ruled for 17 years. They continued with their father's building work and transformed Athens into a beautiful city of marble. In the 5th Century BCE, a golden age emerged in Athens when democracy took place.

However in 490 BCE, Darius 1st , the King of Persia, decided to invade Greece. The Persians had already conquered the Kingdoms of Egypt and Babylonia. The invaders traveled in ships across the Aegean Sea and landed at Marathon on the coast of Attica, just Northeast of Athens. When the Persians attacked on the Plains of Marathon, the heavily armed, Athenian Hopelites won a decisive victory over the Persians. Approximately 6,000 Persians were killed in the Battle of Marathon. Only 192 Athenians perished. Darius was angry and promised to return to Greece to crush their cities and destroy their freedom. The effect of the Greek victory was profound and permanent. Darius died before he could launch another invasion on Greece.

Herodotus was known as the father of Greek History. He was the first person to write what we now call History. He is most famous for his detailed account of the Persian Wars. He traveled widely around the Mediterranean Sea collecting information for his book and brought together a wealth of geographical and anecdotal details about the various peoples involved in the Persian Wars. He was the first person to establish historical facts and write about them as a sequence of linked events.

From 479 BCE, Athens was transformed into a city of glittering marble within 50 years. The Athenians set up an alliance with other city-states on the island of Delos in the Aegean Sea, known as the Delian League after the Persian Wars. They developed a treasury that was kept at the sacred sanctuary of Apollo on Delos. The Delian League turned into an Athenian Empire and Athens entered a golden age of prosperity and freedom.

Pericles, a Statesman and general, was the leader of Athens from 443 BCE to 429 BCE. He was a powerful orator. Pericles was popular with the Athenian citizens and Athens prospered under his rule. Only citizens were allowed a voice in how the state was run.

The Athenians honored and celebrated their gods, who protected their city. The festival of the Goddess Athenia was celebrated with athletic games and with poetry and musical competitions. Sophocles wrote 100 plays. Only 7 plays exist today. He wrote up into his 80s.

Drama was important to the Greeks. They performed on open stages at festivals, comedies and tragedies. Plato, an Athenian philosopher, said, "The city is filled with liberty and free speech and everyone in it is allowed to do as he or she pleases."

The Athenians lived as free citizens and their thriving city attracted Artists, Poets, Historians, Dramatists, Philosophers and Orators from all over Greece.